Dennis Wood
On The Beat
True tales of a former
Manchester Police Officer

P & D Riley

First published June 2005
Reprinted October 2005

P & D Riley
12 Bridgeway East
Runcorn
Cheshire
WA7 6LD
England

ISBN: 1 874712 77 8

British Library Cataloguing in Publication Data
A catalogue record for this book is available from the
British Library

Printed in England.

About the Author

Dennis Wood served in the Manchester Police from 1950 until 1975, a period in which he saw a gradual change from what had been Victorian methods of keeping law and order, to the situation we have today. He entered the police service, as did many of his contemporaries, following military service during and immediately following World War Two.

Married with two sons, Nicholas and Richard, Dennis also writes a column in *Brief*, the monthly journal of the Greater Manchester Police and is well known in the world of after dinner speaking.

His hilarious, authentic tales are typical of a period thought by many law abiding citizens as being halcyon.

The book cover all aspects of the policeman's lot, not least the harsh conditions of service in his day but mainly the necessary humour to put up with it all.

Acknowledgements

The publisher would like to thank Chris Oldham of Greater Manchester Police for permission to use the front cover picture of the author, and to Duncan Broady, curator of Greater Manchester Police Museum for supplying the archive photographs.

Dedication

This book is for my dear, long suffering wife Sylvia

Chapter One

Where the River Irwell fuses with the River Irk, the Romans built their fort and the locals, in their wisdom, nestled around its walls in the hope that the fierce tribes of what was to become Lancashire, might leave them in peace. Now that the protection of Rome has gone, the Lancashire tribes pray that someone will shield them from the descendants of the first Mancunians.

I would like to say that it was the plight of all those needing to be shielded from skulduggery that had influenced my decision to become a guardian of law and order, but rather, it was a remark made by my father, to the effect that following the conclusion of the First World War, there was the Great Depression, which placed everyone out of work, with disastrous consequences. "Except for coppers and people like that," he said. "You can mark my words, history is bound to repeat itself and you lads, unless you've got one of those safe jobs, are going to be in the same boat."

At the headquarters of the Manchester City Police, following an elementary test of knowledge and a fleeting medical examination, I was sworn in as a constable. There was, at that time an acute shortage of recruits throughout the land and providing you were a big strong lad, who had managed to keep away from the courts, you were suitable. Having said that, your first two years were spent as a probationer, during which period a constable's services could be dispensed with without explanation. Once out of that probation it would be difficult to get yourself dismissed.

Firstly there was the training school to be endured. The location was a disused American army camp at Warrington. Nissan huts, a barrack square, a gymnasium and a cook house, reminiscent to most of us of our recently completed service to king and country. Here was great influence paid to teaching the law and its procedures for a gruelling period of three months, after which it became time to launch us upon the citizens of the grimy city.

The allocated number displayed proudly upon the collar of my tunic was B135, indicating that I had become a member of the division covering a large section north of the city centre. For most part it was crowded with small terraced houses and dingy streets, almost all of which sported a pub on the corner. These hostelries, together with the larger establishments to be found dominating the main roads, were, more often than not, the source of our trade, or more precisely their customers were.

On the division we were regarded by the residents as being an army of occupation, constantly interfering with their illegal activities, in answer to which, the iron fist of authority was applied. On the outer limits of the division however, there lived a slightly better class who occupied a more pleasant environment and were more appreciative of our presence.

There were three shifts, called reliefs. Mornings, six a.m. To two p.m. Afternoons, two p.m. to ten p.m. Nights ten p.m. to six a. m. Everyone worked these reliefs on foot, some throughout the whole of their service. The only escape was a transfer to the C.I.D. or to one of very few departments which were in existence in those days. There were a few police vehicles but very limited vacancies to the transport department.

When, after a couple of months, I moved to the better class area of New Moston, I came close to ruining the regard for the police in that district. The local swimming baths, as did many other such council premises, spent the winter months as a dance hall. A plunge would be covered by a sprung dance floor and the surrounding tiled walls cunningly disguised by brightly coloured drapes, altogether a truly professional transformation. It was Christmas Eve and the manager had requested that the officer on the night relief put in an appearance around midnight in order that any rowdiness would be nipped in the bud. In those happier times, the mere presence of a helmet was normally sufficient to prevent disorderliness. The beat covering the area was territorially the size of three or four beats in the less tranquil districts nearer to the city and the beat man was obliged to make use of an allocated bicycle, in order to properly patrol.

At about ten thirty, having pedalled through a biting wind which had threatened to dismount me throughout the uphill journey from Newton Heath to the lone mecca of entertainment,

I was able to introduce myself to the dance hall manager.

"Thank God you're here," he whispered. "There's a crowd of lads from Failsworth who've got passouts and gone across to the pub over the road. A couple of the staff say they will come back later and cause trouble."

His voice, in a series of nervous shrieks, amplified against the efforts of a four piece band further within the premises. I reassured him that I would return in time to deal with any intentions on behalf of unruly youths and left to visit the rest of the beat, mainly in the hope that some resident or other, filled with festive spirit would kindly invite me in to their abode to sample a mince pie and a glass or two of good cheer. By a quarter to midnight, no such benevolence having materialised, I cycled back to the baths.

When I passed through the entrance hall the band was struggling with the national anthem and there was a general stampede from the dance floor, along a corridor, to an area from which some of the clientele appeared to be collecting their coats. The group of youths had returned from smelling the barmaid's apron a couple of minutes prior to my arrival and the manager, on observing my approach, plucked up the courage to deny them entry. "The dancing is over, so you can't come in," he yelled at the leader of the pack, a large ginger haired individual.

I gripped the lout by his neck and tossed him down the steps. The rest left like quiet little lambs and I turned to find the shaking manager attempting to regain order along the corridor. "They won't queue for their bloody coats properly," he shrieked. I looked past him into a room similar to the dance hall and could see that everyone had crowded along the nearside wall at the end of which was a small cloakroom.

"Why don't you get them to form an orderly line across the whole room, snake like, then they can retrieve their coats without all this crush?" I shouted. His reaction was to stare at me with the expression of a man who had abandoned all hope of ever controlling anything again and I was becoming fed up with the whole affair and Christmas in general.

Now, if I was ever to get out of the place, something would have to be done. I shoved my way into the seething mass and yelled at them to spread out across the floor, at the same time heaving those nearest to me further into the empty space, a space which turned out to be a plunge filled with water. No wonder they had been confining themselves to one end of the room, which I had assumed was another dancing area. The sounds of splashing and howls of protest ringing in my ears, I quit the building. Outside, from behind some bushes I could see those who had taken to the water, the ladies in their finery and their escorts in appropriate suits, dripping and splashing towards their several homes. It had, by good fortune, been the shallow end of the pool which had claimed them, so that no real harm had been done. I remained on that nice quiet beat for a further four weeks then moved back into the more iniquitous sections of the division.

In no time, I had readjusted to the routine of trying to minimise the plethora of wrongdoing which obtained amongst the masses dwelling in the run down districts. "You've got to keep laughing son," said the old copper I was assisting with the body of a man, found dead in a flea ridden lodging house. I taking the head and shoulders, he the feet, we carried the poor unfortunate down one of those awkward staircases, still to be found in Victorian properties. I made an effort to follow his advice but when he left me to remove the lice laden garments of the corpse and lay it out in the station mortuary, I was unable to raise the slightest titter.

The officer in question, I later discovered, was well known for his practical jokes, not least the coal yard jape. Behind the gas works was a large coal yard from which local coal retailers would collect their requirements, bag it, and deliver to their customers. A bustling place by day, at night deserted, save for an ancient watchman, who, in an effort to supplement his income, devised a sort of haven for the flotsam and jetsam of life.

He fixed a stout rope at one end of the yard and drew it around a hook at the opposite wall. Tramps and ordinary drunks, on payment of sixpence per night, could drape themselves over the rope by tucking it under their armpits, and in that posture, more or less pass a blissful night's sleep. That would be, if the joker wasn't on nights, as his bit of amusement was to undo the rope from its hook, thereby casting the sleeping beauties to the coal dust beneath them. As the shouts and curses reached crescendo the constable would be strolling innocently, on his beat half a mile away.

The divisional headquarters for the city centre, overlooked an extensive square which was the façade of the elegant town hall. There, amongst those of other past dignitaries, stood an impressive effigy of the late Prince Albert. No reverence was ever paid to the statue by the hundreds of pigeons abiding in the square, nor for that matter, to the crowds of humans who traversed the paving there. Sergeant Bullford, a well known figure at the station, eased his mighty frame from the charge office chair and struggled to the public kiosk in answer to a persistent ringing of the bell there. He had despatched the clerk to prepare a mug of tea and was now obliged to perform that officer's duty. At first sight the kiosk was occupied by nothing more than a pigeon, then there appeared a small scruffy lad around eight years old. "Please sir, it's 'urt. It's got run over or summat." said the boy, who then shot off.

The sergeant, seeing that the bird had indeed suffered a broken wing, carried it through to the station yard, where placing it gently down, stamped on the creature and relieved it from its misery. The culling, unknown to Sergeant Bullford, had been witnessed by two detectives from the window of the C.I.D. room above the yard. The deceased having been committed to a dustbin, the sergeant repaired to his office chair. The Criminal Investigation Department and the uniform branch are historically in opposition to each other, with little love lost between either, and any opportunity for one faction to get one over on the other was always taken with enthusiasm. The detectives, having ascertained from the clerk the facts of the case, and the clerk, a Judas in that he despised the sergeant almost as much as detectives, agreeing to go along with a plot they were hatching, the die was cast.

About half an hour later, the sergeant answered the telephone. The cultured tone of the caller was received respectfully. "I am the Duke of Cambridge," the caller announced, with such a tone of authority as to bring the sergeant to his feet. "Now you may believe, as many do, a pigeon fancier is some common fellow who wears a cloth cap, but that is not so. I in fact am a leading figure in the world of pigeons." Bullford, sensing disaster, and with a throat which had completely dried, asked how he might be of assistance.

"Actually, my chauffeur drove the rolls through Albert Square today, and as he did so, my prize pigeon, Lady Charlotte, flew out of the window. Before the fellow was able to park he was on the other side of the town. However, he did discover that a small boy had found my little beauty and had handed it in at your station, to a big fat ugly sergeant with a red nose. I have instructed someone to collect my little darling later today." At that 'his grace' hung up. Sergeant Bullford slid back into his chair and fought for his breath as he attempted to think through a red mist.

He began by calling every officer on duty, in to the station and ordered them to the square. "Take your capes and grab as many bloody pigeons as you can find, bring 'em back here to me in the yard. Now get going," he bellowed. If one could be found that was identical to Lady Charlotte's corpse he stood a chance of getting away with it. At first, all the officers set about the task with enthusiasm, after all it was a change from routine, and they were soon queuing in the yard with their feathered prisoners. Bullford, having exhumed the dead bird from the bin, held it at arm's length whilst the constables filed past with their examples. The first batch, having failed to qualify, were released, and the officers returned to the square for another intake. Shoppers, office workers on lunchtime break, and foreign visitors, tarried to enjoy the spectacle of a dozen or so burly coppers running about and trying to catch playful pigeons in their capes.

One party of Japanese business men, believing that it was some ritual similar to the changing of the guard at Buckingham Palace, set about recording the whole thing on their myriad of cameras. The ebb and flow of feathered detainees, some making their second or third visit, continued for a further two hours, all with negative effect. When it was time for the sergeant and the relief to go home, the matter had been given up as a bad job. Cycling homewards, the seriousness of the situation preoccupied the hapless sergeant to the extent that when a drunken youth staggered from the kerb and into his path, he merely rode on, when in normal circumstances he would have belted him around the ears.

The next morning, at the station he spent a miserable couple of hours awaiting the arrival of the duke. He had been awake most of the night rehearsing his explanation, and each attempt seemed to be weaker than its predecessor. At one o'clock, the bell of the public kiosk was operated, and with a heavy heart he moved to answer it. There was no sign of anyone, but on the counter was a pigeon and nearby was a note. 'Dear sergeant,' it read. 'I am so sorry to have inconvenienced you. When I returned to my mansion I discovered that Lady Charlotte had returned to her loft, quite unharmed. In fact it is she who is delivering this missive to you. Would you be so kind as to take her outside and release her. She will find her own way home.'

Sergeant Bullford complied with the request. At least, in part he did.

Chapter Two

A few weeks following the unfortunate affair of the dancing bathers, I began a tour of duty at the Cheetham Hill section station. The area had been the retreat of business and professional people throughout Victoria's reign and their imposing dwellings had been made into flats to accommodate the less affluent. A busy main thoroughfare, bounded by retail outlets, ran through the section on its way from the city centre to Prestwich and to Bury. It being long before there were any supermarkets, it was a popular shopping area, where, particularly on Saturdays, crowds of people filled the pavements on both sides of the road.

The morning relief, beginning as it did at six o'clock, saw little of those seething masses, or indeed, anyone at all. I was gradually getting to know other probationers and making friends of them. There was some unwritten law which, for some peculiar reason, banned officers who had left their probation behind and had been therefore accepted on a permanent basis, from holding any form of conversation with anyone with less than two years service. Sergeants and above, forced to speak in order to convey an instruction, went a step further in considering a probationer to be something offensive they had picked up on the sole of their boot.

On my first morning on the Cheetham Hill section I lined up with another five constables for the parade. This was a ritual at which the Section Sergeant required to see what were called your appointments. Everyone had to hold up to view, a truncheon, notebook, handcuffs, whistle and a dog lead then replace them to several pockets in their uniform. The sergeant would then allocate the beats, the times to come in and any special duties appertaining to a particular beat. At the commencement of that morning's ceremony, I was aware that a heavily built man, much taller than myself, had entered the room and had taken up a position at my side. The newcomer was in plain clothes, with a black full length overcoat and trilby hat. He had produced a notebook which was of an official nature like the rest of us, but one which could be obtained at any newsagent's.

I formed the opinion that this officer was there for some sort of duty that required him to be incognito for some reason, and when the sergeant told him to patrol as usual, he feverishly scribbled in his book.

The parade having been completed, we all walked out of the station towards our respective beats and I found that the plain clothes officer was strolling at my side. He made no conversation, which I put down to the fact that he being some ten years older than myself, was observing the unwritten rule. I was surprised, when reaching my beat and turning away from him to hear him speak for the first time. "Bleedin' Heaton Park again," he said as he turned away to begin a trek of some three miles towards that huge expanse of recreational tranquillity.

The mysterious stranger was at the station when we were signed off at two o'clock and I heard him inform the sergeant that he had nothing to report. He turned up again the next day and I asked a new found pal, P.C. John Barlow, a fellow probationer, to fill me in on him. "Oh, Humphrey you mean?" laughed John. "He's a nutter who lives round the back here with his old mother. He's been parading with the morning relief every day for years. Goes to the park and walks round till its time to come in at two." On reflection, he wasn't doing any harm and may have being doing some good.

The day following I left the station with P.C. Barlow and as we were on adjacent beats, strolled with him in the direction of our allocations. He informed me that he had been fortunate enough to find a flat nearby in which to live until a police house became available. "The wife will be still asleep but if we are quiet we can have a quick cuppa," he said. We crept into hallway and deposited our capes and helmets on the hall table, then to the kitchen for the promised refreshment. Five minutes later we collected our capes and helmets from the hall and with a quickened pace set off towards the point of parting. It was fast becoming light and the heavy clouds which had been hidden in the darkness were now, it appeared, at rooftop height. As we prepared to part, the forerunner of what was to be a full morning of heavy rain began to fall. I took my cape from my shoulder, unfolded it and with a flourish, swung it around my shoulders. It was a piece of equipment used by police forces since eighteen twenty nine and its closely woven cloth guaranteed protection from the worst of deluges for many hours. By the time I had fastened the buttons on the garment the downpour had begun in earnest. I was surprised to see that John's cape was still resting on his shoulder and that he had made no attempt to wear it. "I've picked up the wife's bloody skirt from the hall by mistake!" he said as he turned to retrace his steps to the Barlow household.

I was beginning to realise that those earlier months spent at the training centre were little more than a brief and misleading introduction to a job which had to be learned in the school of experience. I was approached one morning by a man on a bicycle, who informed me that there had been an accident on Oldham Road and that a little girl had been taken to the dead house. The small group of locals parted to allow me through to a car which was parked half way on to the pavement and where its driver, ashen faced, leaned over the bonnet in obvious distress. Everyone began talking at the same time, putting forward their version of the occurrence. "I was stood at the bus stop here and saw this car hit the girl when she ran into the road," puffed a stout woman. "Two men picked her up and I went round to tell her mother that she had been taken in the dead house and that's where her mother went," explained another spectator.

Fatal accident reports, on behalf of the Coroner, were always conducted by the sergeants and with that in mind I asked a local shopkeeper to let me use his telephone. "There's been a young girl killed by a car sir," I informed the Inspector at the divisional headquarters, giving the location. He instructed me to remain at the scene until the sergeant arrived and not to say anything to the driver. "Get the particulars of as many witnesses as possible and hand them to Sergeant Dickinson when he gets there."

Sergeant Dickinson was one of those supervisors who struck fear into probationers, with his bouts of vile temper, triggered as they were, by the slightest error on behalf of any such constable under his command. On this morning, having to leave a breakfast of two eggs, a pile of bacon, beans and fried bread, after only one mouthful, in order to cycle a mile uphill and deal with a report which would take the rest of the day to complete irritated him to the point of explosion. His expletive outburst on my greeting him dispersed the small gathering and any newcomer could have been excused for believing that it was I who had killed the poor girl. As I handed him the list of potential witnesses and listened to a tirade on a wasted breakfast, he had his back towards the Prince Of Wales pub. I, on the other hand, had a full view of the group of people leaving by its main door, one of whom was a girl of some ten or eleven years wearing a bandage around her knee and bathing in what was more attention and sympathy than she had hitherto experienced.

"She's all right," said the motorist, speaking for the first time and pointing to the casualty for which he had been responsible. The sergeant glanced behind then back at me. "You reported to the inspector that the kid had been taken off to the mortuary," he yelled, his face changing from a deep crimson hue to purple.

"Everyone said she had been taken to the dead house and I assumed they meant an ambulance had taken her to the mortuary. I mean everyone was saying it sarge."

"I dare say they did," he screamed. "That's what the bloody Prince Of Wales is known as round here." He leapt on his bike and sped off in the hope that the canteen staff had not yet got round to throwing his breakfast away and I carried on with the report. On the occasion of Sergeant Dickinson's retirement party many years later, I reminded him of the dead house misunderstanding and enquired whether in fact he was in time to rescue the meal. He told me to perform a feat which I would have found an anatomical impossibility had I attempted it!

I always detested Sunday duties. Walking along deserted streets on a beat which covered a small area for eight hours could be boring in the extreme, especially as it always seemed to be raining. On one such evening whilst examining shop doors to ascertain whether or not their owners had remembered to lock them, I heard the clanging of an intruder alarm and found it to be that of an old fashioned drapery business in the next block. Most of these premises were known as live on, in that their proprietors occupied accommodation on the upper and rear floors. I knocked at the main door at the same time flashing my lamp at the window above. The window was duly opened and the shopkeeper, a woman of mature years, enquired what it was I wanted.

"Can't you hear your alarm ringing? Come down and let me make sure you are all right," I called.

I stood for some ten minutes, the rain dripping from my cape on to my knees and washing my boots, listening to what I later discovered were seven keys being turned in seven locks on the shop door. When at long last the door was opened I was confronted by a tiny woman, whose attire was reminiscent of photographs I had seen depicting Queen Victoria. It was with some reluctance on her part that I was invited into the shop and through to the living quarters at the rear. The keys, with which she had released the locks, hung on a long chain around her neck and rattled as she moved. She returned to the shop and re-locked the door leaving me to partly dry off before the welcome glow of the fireplace.

"Well, everything is in order, the rain probably set your alarm off, so I'll let you get to bed," I said.

"I can't let you out until you have arrested those people who keep coming down the chimney and pinching stuff from the shop," she shrieked, clutching the chain of keys to her breast. I attempted to reason with her to no avail and finding there was no telephone on the premises I became a little concerned. I had been missing from my beat for an hour and the Section Sergeant might be looking for me.

"There's one of 'em now. Over there behind the couch, go on arrest him," she screamed. I went to the area she had pointed out and took hold of the invisible intruder going through the motions of a violent struggle, during which an expensive vase and a stuffed owl in a glass cover were smashed. I dragged her imaginary burglar into the shop area and demanded that she opened the door.

"Not yet, I want you to give 'im a good hiding first," she shouted, obviously carried away by the pantomime. I went through the motions of thumping the imaginary thief for a few seconds then further demanded to be released in order to get him to the station. "Only if you both promise to go to Sunday school," she said and I found myself promising on behalf of both of us.

Only then was the long ceremony of the keys performed, allowing me to hurry off to the station. I was fifteen minutes late for signing off and the inspector on nights demanded an excuse. He was a well known disciplinarian and I could see that he was ready to put me on paper, so it was with a heavy heart that I related the events of the evening.

The inspector produced a loud laugh. "Miss Sudlow claims another victim," he roared, slapping the desk with his huge hand. I wished him goodnight and went home.

During the months which followed, I witnessed the coming and going of a great many probationers, either because they failed to reach the standard or because they had become disenchanted with the job in general, or the poor pay. Often the reason for leaving was because a wife or girlfriend objected to the shift work.

An officer who was working at Cheetham Hill during my own stint there seemed to be just the type to be a policeman. Six feet two and broad shouldered, he certainly looked the part. What set him apart from the rest were his cultured tones and obvious privileged education. Harold, as he was called, confided in me one night, saying that he had joined the bobbies merely as a stepping stone to better things. "I was demobbed a few months ago after serving in Burma as a captain in the Lancashire Fusiliers," he said. "I had intended to help with my father's antique business up in the lakes, but after several arguments I moved down here and found a little flat. I have been applying for managerial posts." he went on to explain. A couple of nights later, whilst in the station, he informed me that he had been successful in getting an interview at a well known soap manufacturer's at Liverpool.

"The problem is that they want to see me next Wednesday and my day off is on Thursday," he said.

The ancient station officer, who had been eavesdropping, shoved his huge head between us. "Change your day off," he said.

"He'd have to put a report in to do that and if I know anything about it the sergeant would say it can't be arranged," I said, speaking in the voice of experience.

"No! no! just pop in and explain to the chief superintendent, that you're off tomorrow. Go and see him in the morning," insisted the station officer.

I had misgivings, particularly as I had come to know what a bastard the old copper was. He enjoyed immense pleasure in letting the sergeants and inspectors know what the constables were doing, resulting in many being caught doing whatever it happened to be. Some time later I learned the outcome of the captain's foray into the unknown from the charge office clerk.

It has to be said, that so frequently were men resigning after a short period of service there was little opportunity for supervising officers to become familiar with a face.

"This very smartly dressed bloke walked in to the charge

16

office and told the inspector he wanted to see the chief superintendent immediately," said the clerk. The divisional headquarters, lying as it did in the centre of the scruffiest location of the force area, the inspector became temporarily disarmed by the posh accent and smart togs before him. He telephoned the boss and informed him of the distinguished visitor, suggesting that he see him. His observation that he could be from the Home Office determined the issue, as he had a vague recollection of reading about a surprise visit to another force, which caught everyone with their pants round their ankles.

Harold was directed to the top office, where Chief Superintendent Dan Drummond rose to greet him. "Ingham," said the stranger, as he took the proffered hand. He was asked to take a seat and invited to take a cup of tea, which was dutifully brought from the canteen by the clerk, who after puffing his way up three flights of stairs with it, discovered that the recipient didn't take milk and was obliged to carry out the whole exercise again. For a while the conversation was on the weather and cricket, a preamble employed by the chief, in an effort to weigh up his visitor, who, to his annoyance, lit a cigarette as he sprawled back in an easy chair.

"Now sir, how can I be of assistance?" the booming voice, rich with the tone of its Scottish heritage enquired. The constable leaned forward and announced, with an air of strict confidentiality, that he was to appear before the board of a large concern in Liverpool next Wednesday and that his day off was unfortunately on Thursday. He fell to silence and stared at his host, who, from beneath a pair of bushy unruly eyebrows, stared fiercely back at him. A sneaking suspicion haunted the senior officer, one which he was unable to put his finger on for a moment.

"Can I ask you if you have any connection with the police in any way?" he enquired.

"Well yes, of course, I am P.C. Ingham, we met when I joined the division a couple of months ago," replied Harold. To say that the Chief Superintendent was upset, was to put it mildly.

"You could hear him downstairs in the charge office," was the clerk's account of it. The inspector ran up the stairs three at a time to find out what the yelling and cursing was about, to be passed half way by the fleeing captain.

There followed a kind of interview with the inspector, which was designed to leave him in no doubt as to his future pros-

17

pects should he ever repeat such a miscalculation. Captain Ingham never disclosed the identity of his advisor in the affair and indeed his day off was changed as requested. He was successful in his appointment to the soap company and was allowed to resign without having to serve the normal four weeks notice. That move was apparently made in order to get rid of him before the indignity became common knowledge, a move which sadly, or happily, depending who you were, failed.

Chapter Three

I came to the end of my period of probation and was accepted as a permanent member of the force. I had been consistent in capturing a great number of serious wrongdoers, burglars, car and sundry thieves. Of course, as is often the case, it was a matter of being in the right place at the right time and very often being somewhere where you shouldn't be. I have nipped along a quiet entry to relieve myself, to find someone clambering out over the very yard door I was peeing against, with a sack of goods stolen from the shop within.

Sometimes I have walked through my beat at night, and been overcome with a pressing desire to go to some premises well out of my way, and arrested thieves I have discovered in those premises. Time and again that sort of phenomenon has occurred and I have no explanation for it. These incidents, together with the arrests for minor things, like drunkenness, assault, begging etc., gained me a great deal of experience both at the Magistrates' Court and the Quarter Sessions, later to be the Crown Court. These experiences prompted me to begin studying the criminal law in earnest which built up my confidence and self esteem. As soon as I was allowed to, I passed the examinations which qualified a constable to become a sergeant. An achievement which, sadly, does not mean that one would be automatically promoted.

There were those who had not the slightest interest in promotion, being content to get through to their pension with the minimum effort. The basic duty of a constable is the protection of life and property and unless it can be proved that an individual officer was failing to perform those duties, the authorities must retain him. Who is to say that a police officer that never arrests or summonses anyone, is not carrying out the protection of life and property? Who can prove that as he walks along the street, his presence hasn't put off someone lying in wait for a prospective rape victim, or his examination of a row of shops, hasn't dissuaded burglars?. Providing such a none industrious officer does nothing foolish, like becoming drunk on duty, or committing a crime, he should sail through his service and leave with an exemplary character.

Police Constable Charlie Rothschild, was a perfect example of an officer determined to complete his period of office in that way and when I first came across him, he had managed to do it for twenty years. He was of distinguished appearance and you may well believe that he was a distant relative of that wealthy family whose name he bore. At a time when none of his colleagues could drive a vehicle, let alone own one, he could be found driving cars belonging to one or other of the many ladies of his acquaintance.

In his travels he would visit pubs and social clubs in outlying districts well away from the force area and where suitable, would arrange for coach trips, always avoiding the disclosure that we were the police, by mentioning that we were a rugby club or something of that nature. These outings, by coach, always took place on a Saturday, encompassing the change over of duties from mornings to nights, as the whole relief would be free from Saturday at 2 p.m. until Sunday at 10 p.m.

The first of many such excursions involved the trippers rendezvousing at a pub on the division at 5 p.m. I was one of the first to arrive and in view of the limited period of time between getting home and turning up, I decided to remain dressed in police trousers, blue uniform shirt, black tie and a sports jacket, which I had been given at the time of demobilisation from His Majesty's Forces. As each of the others turned up it was apparent that they also had been pressed for time and had decided on the same outfit as myself.

The trips were always something of a mystery tour to preserve secrecy and on this initial occasion, we found ourselves in the ancient town of Chester. The Baron had arranged an evening meal at a first class hotel, to be followed with a knees up at a nearby beer house. All thirty three of us were seated at a long banqueting table in a richly appointed dining room and Charles, who unlike the rest of us, was dressed immaculately in a grey suit with shirt and sporty tie, left us for the cocktail bar.

The head waiter, looking down his long nose at the rest of us, caused the soup course to be served. Now many of the officers present had been in the force since the nineteen thirties and had never dined in a good class restaurant before. One old copper, slurping his soup, grasped the tails of the head waiter's coat and called out, "fetch some more bleeding bread." There were many other demonstrations of missing table manners, accompanied by ribald comments directed toward the waitresses and the look on the face of the head waiter said it all.

He went in to the bar between courses and complained to the staff there. "I have no idea who this lot are, but I've never served a more disgusting mob in my career," he said.

"I'm afraid they are with me," said the Baron, as he replaced his gin and lime on the bar counter. "They are all inmates at the Springfield Mental Home in Manchester. I'm the manager and I am treating them to a day out." The head waiter apologised and said that he now understood. Following the meal we all left the hotel and trooped in to a small pub across the road where someone ordered thirty two pints and a gin and lime. The landlord, taken unawares by such a large influx as early as this, called his wife to assist him and to get the barmaid to come in. Half way through the frantic production of the beer, someone enquired as to the location of the piano. "There's no music nor singing in Chester pubs," smirked the licensee and we all marched out to the coach, leaving them still pulling away.

Our driver knew of a pub in Ellesmere Port where there was singing and we were driven there at speed. It was as rough a place as could be found anywhere in the world and the clientele resembled the crew of one of those pirate ships which once roamed the oceans. At least there was a piano and after some of our party had put a few of the snarling customers in their place, we settled down to a jolly night's entertainment.

There followed many more trips to a variety of drinking establishments and we all attended regularly, some times posing as the Newton Heath Rugby Club or the Strangeways Old Boys and only on one occasion in our true capacity, to a club a long way from home, where on discovering that the bar always closed at eleven, the Baron, giving the committee the impression that he was the chief constable, wrote out the granting of an extension until midnight on the back of an old betting slip he had found in his pocket. In the course of time wages improved and people were able to own their own transport, in which they could visit those far away places, and the Baron's coach trips became a thing of the past.

Cheetham Hill, as I have mentioned before, was an extremely busy shopping area and one Saturday afternoon as I squeezed myself through the crowds, I noticed the wife of a local licensee, laden with shopping bags who was elbowing her way into my direction. Mary, as she was named, was well known to the local constabulary as most of their celebrations were held at the pub. She prepared the buffets on those occasions and having a lot of experience with regards to the appetites of policemen, she did an excellent job.

As she drew close to me I took her by the arm. "You're under arrest," I said and gently propelled her towards the nearby station, where I intended to make her a cup of tea. Mary, who knew me well and loved a joke, walked with me into the station without a word.

"Hello Mary, got you at last have we," laughed the station officer, as we passed him and into the dining room. She declined the proffered tea and spoke for the first time. "I think you've mistaken me for my sister," she said. "I'm Winifred, Mary Smythe is my twin sister." She picked up her shopping and left the station and it was some months later that I saw Mary at the pub. Winifred was there too and any thoughts I had entertained that Mary was having me on were dismissed immediately as they were truly identical. Fortunately everyone saw the funny side of it and I was forgiven. It was yet another lesson.

Among the few civilians who were employed by the police were those who operated the divisional switchboards. Most divisional headquarters had a system of land lines to police boxes and metal pillars which were sited at strategic points and fitted with a blue lamp which could be operated to draw the attention of the beat man to the fact that the telephonist had a message for him. The operators were adept in dealing with minor matters, though anything of importance would be put through to the inspector. One of those minor matters was in connection with a book, held in the telephone

21

om, which contained details of time in lieu accumulated by officers working overtime, for example court appearances. No overtime money was paid and any overtime had to be taken as time in lieu by applying at the commencement of the shift. These applications were made to the Section Sergeant, who in turn would pass them on to the switchboard. The total of time due in the book was then passed to the Charge Office Inspector, together with the application and he would decide whether you could go off early or not. The inspector's decision was final and would be conveyed to the applicant by the telephonist, who would then adjust the book accordingly.

One of these operators was a weasel like man of some thirty years of age, who had one of those faces you could never tire of hitting, though he was very popular with the charge office staff. He resided close to the station and though some commodities like tea and sugar were still on ration, he regularly supplied the office with them, donated by his mother. On one of those rainy dark evenings in winter I had been side-tracked by a domestic dispute and was late getting to where I should have been. I decided to double back on my beat and as I moved through a dark entry at the rear of a large grocery shop I saw a shadowy figure coming out of the yard gate and carrying a bundle over its shoulder.

I reached into the pocket of my cumbersome greatcoat and pulled out my torch just as the figure took off at high speed. I instinctively threw the heavy instrument and heard it smash, to the accompaniment of a loud squeal of pain. Encumbered by the greatcoat I dismissed all thought of running after the miscreant and instead set about recovering the shattered torch and sack of groceries. Having later reported the incident and returned the goods to their rightful owner, I forgot the whole thing. At the end of that fortnight of nights I changed over to the afternoon relief and on the first day, as I paraded for duty, I asked the sergeant if I could make use of time in lieu and go off four hours early. The sergeant returned from phoning the switch to inform me that I had used up all my time due.

As I have said, I was never away from court and knew that there was some thirty hours to which I was entitled. I was also aware of the futility of arguing with supervising officers and resigned myself to remaining on duty. It took a long time to build up my time again and this time I recorded every minute of it in the back pages of my note book.

Whilst I was on afternoons, my colleague Taff Williams, was on nights. At the end of his shift he cycled home through the darkened back streets of the division. The Co-operative Stores which lay on his route, was lit on the interior by a bulb of some low wattage as a security measure and as he rode past he caught a fleeting glimpse of a figure inside the store. He cycled to the rear of the premises and quietly dismounted. He stood in the dark passage for a while and was rewarded by the appearance of a figure which struggled under the weight of a laden sack.

The intruder, brought to the front of the shop and placed under the glow of a street lamp, revealed itself to be the obnoxious telephonist from police headquarters, his heavy burden being tea, sugar and other rationed foodstuffs, bound to be sold amongst his neighbours. In the charge office, Taff was made to feel that he was the villain of the piece, due to the fact that tea and sugar was going to be in short supply henceforth. It goes without saying that the office staff were unaware of their benefactor's nefarious activities, but to allay any such suggestion being made in a court, the burglar was sacked and not charged.

It had been a thief's paradise, knowing the whereabouts of every policeman over a huge area and that as the beats changed over, there was a temporary absence of cover. Of course I was unable to prove who it was that had crossed all my time due out of the book, though I did later discover that the weasel was off sick for a week following the beat lamp incident .

Chapter Four

Throughout the nineteen fifties, police pay was dismally poor and it was not uncommon for officers to supplement their incomes by moonlighting. It was a disciplinary offence to carry out a second employment and such activity had to be closely guarded. One avenue popular amongst police officers was that of the funeral trade, including pallbearers, drivers and some mortuary work. Spotting half a dozen of one's colleagues officiating at a funeral was common when patrolling the beat and the practise seemed to escape the knowledge of senior officers for years.

Many places of worship, once heavily patronised, had fallen into disuse and despite the building of vast housing estates in their close proximity, congregations had dwindled to a handful. Where each establishment once sported a clergyman of its own, now made do with a cleric looking after several churches at a time. One such church on the division held a large graveyard in which there were many family graves and tombs dating back throughout the nineteenth and early twentieth centuries.

On a drizzly November morning, the deceased octogenarian Matilda Chambers, was carried from a brief service in the draughty church to be set down for a moment at the side of the open family grave. The undertaker and his team of incognito coppers, passed the ropes under the coffin and eased it over in readiness to lower it slowly at the vicar's signal. The grave digger yawned and slipped away for a smoke and the fine drizzle penetrated the clothing of those present. There was a fair crowd of mourners as the old lady's family once owned a cotton mill nearby, at which many of those present and their parents before them, earned a meagre living.

The constables took the strain and began to lower the coffin. The vicar intoned the appropriate passages from his prayer book and as the casket reached the waiting earth, the solemnity was shattered by the ear splitting shriek of one of the female mourners. "That's the wrong bloody grave," she yelled. "You're putting her in the wrong grave I tell yer."

The visibly shaken clergyman dropped the prayer book, which was recovered when the 'moonlighters' hauled the coffin to the surface and on to the edge of the grave, at which stage one of the officers slipped on the wet surface and fell into the hole so recently vacated by the deceased lady. But not before grabbing the cassock of the vicar for support and consequently pulling him down into the void with him.

An elderly mourner, being familiar with the surroundings, pointed out the genuine repository of the family and announced that the family had been interred there for over a century to his knowledge. The man of cloth, having been pulled out of the grave, along with the officer, declared, over the profanities of his temporary companion, that the service

24

would be curtailed for two hours until the graves were sorted out.

The undertaker announced that he and his staff were leaving in order to do another funeral and would be returning in time to deal with the matter. The mourners declined an invitation to take a cup of tea in the crumbling church hall and instead, flocked to a nearby pub. The parson, scraping large deposits of mud from his regalia, informed the grave digger that he was required to open the newly designated grave, at which he threatened to down tools unless he was paid extra in advance. The furious cleric was obliged to stump up the money from his own pocket and the work commenced.

On the return of the undertaker, one of the off duty policemen was sent to the pub in order to get the mourners back. A couple of the moonlighters, including the messenger, had been recognised by several of the assembly, and two hours of steady drinking had led the blame at the feet of the constabulary.

After a deal of arguing and threats to thump one or two of them, a fair percentage staggered back to the burial ground. The fresh start went reasonably well and even the rain left off for a time. The old lady, hopefully unaware of the events, at last lay at rest amongst her family. The mourners went back to the pub and rejoined those who, through drink, had been unable to attend the second ceremony and the moonlighters went home to enjoy a few hours sleep, before getting themselves ready for the night shift.

Gradually, the business of building great empires within the force took on its early stages. Departments that already existed took on extra staff, augmented by civilians, whilst new and bizarre departments seemed to be being born every week. One such innovation was the Accident Prevention Department, which had an office in police headquarters and on each division a constable, whose duty it was to instruct the public as to how they might avoid being run over.

Of course, the majority of us, working shifts, entertained the hope that we would be chosen for one or other of those cushy numbers, on nine to five with each weekend off and it was with some incredulity that the choice of officer for our division was a man who, barely out of his probation, was considered by everyone, public alike, to be a first class idiot.

I was once dealing with a matter which involved the assistance of a male nurse at a local hospital for the mentally ill

25

and was accompanied by the future Accident Prevention Officer. Out of the constable's hearing the nurse said, "How do you get on with that bloke officer?" I said that I had not had much to do with him and asked, "why?"

"Well I've had a great deal to do with these things and he has maniacal eyes. I can't say what type of mania, but take it from me, that's what he's got mate," he said. He asked me not to repeat his remarks to my colleague and I never did.

This then was the police officer who was to keep accidents to a minimum and on his first day in that important post he paraded at the station from whence he was directed to a school some three miles away. He had been permitted to journey about on his motor scooter and to wear a civilian raincoat over his uniform, whilst carrying his helmet in a pannier of the machine.

He sped away from the station and down the long hill which would bring him to the traffic lights before turning off into the direction of the eagerly awaiting scholars. The signals changed to red and he applied the brakes, to no avail. The scooter hurtled on towards the junction and made straight for an elderly man, who, having done so before on hundreds of occasions, assumed he could cross to the opposite pavement whilst the lights were on green in his favour.

The accident prevention expert, somehow, pulled the scooter over to the left, and actually only shunted the old boy with the rear wheel, sending him rolling across to his intended destination. Passers by summoned an ambulance and the pedestrian was carted off to have treatment for shock and a fractured ankle. The accident, having involved a police officer, fell into the category of the report having to be prepared by a sergeant, who quickly discovered that the officer's driving licence had long expired and that there was no insurance in respect of the scooter!

A mechanical examination revealed that the vehicle was devoid of brakes. The constable went off sick and was told not to discuss the matter with a living soul, but in spite of his strict compliance with that instruction, the story was gleefully spread around the force within the hour. A few gentlemen of the press, normally the natural enemy of the police, were somehow informed and turned up at the home of the hapless officer.

Apart from unavoidably having his photograph taken, he declined to assist them and their story in the publications the

26

next day left nothing to the imagination.

The accident prevention officer was relieved of his post after a brief appearance at court on a Saturday when the press tend to be absent and maximum publicity can be avoided. To the bewilderment of all, he was then appointed to another nine to five job, that of clerk in the newly formed Public Relations Branch, where he remained until he retired many years later. The only saving grace.

There was no shortage of odd characters like the accident prevention officer on the division and I suppose it would be a dull world without them. The new recruit I was detailed to show round on a sunny evening seemed to be the type who would keep law and order on any beat once the rough edges had been worn off. He was around twenty three years of age, well over six feet tall, with a face that looked as if someone had been chopping fire wood on it over a long period of time.

All probationers tended to reveal a great deal about themselves during their first few months, then spend the next twenty eight years wishing they hadn't! One of the shortcomings related to these confessions, is to become saddled with a nickname, which stays until death. This young man entertained me with stories of his prowess in the ring when he was carrying out his national service in the navy. "Fought 'em all," he said, smashing his right fist into the palm of his left hand, an action which caused a couple of approaching youths to cross to the other side of the street. "Was the middleweight champion of the fleet until I came out this year," he went on. I began to warm to the lad, particularly when we turned a corner to find a group of men, full of beer and squaring up to each other.

"Get off home you lot," the probationer said, thrusting his battle scarred face into the crowd. All the assembled broke up and quietly complied with the officer's instruction, leaving the footpath cleared for our progress round the beat. My relating the incident to colleagues the next day, resulted in the young officer becoming, 'Basher Molloy'.

About this time, a new chief constable was appointed who, having spent a short period reorganising everything, found time for relaxation. He had been informed that there was a champion fighter within the ranks and in the knowledge that his former force held a boxing tournament annually and that the event was only six weeks away, he informed its organisers that he would be entering his Manchester challenger.

The pugilist selected as the basher's opponent was considered in his own force, to be impregnable, or at least one would require to be armed with a sledge hammer in order to hurt him.

The chief sent for Basher Molloy and told him of the arrangements he had made and how much he was looking forward to the contest and the faces of his former colleagues when their champion, who had reigned for so long, suffered a humiliating defeat in his hands. He could see that Basher had a great deal of experience, but realised that there should be a period of training in order to bring him to tip top condition.

"I will inform your division that you will not be doing any duties for the next few weeks. Instead, you must spend that period of time in strict training," said the chief. Basher disappeared as far as we were concerned, though rough details of what was taking place filtered through as rumours.

"He's resigned," said one officer, who lived near the champ. "Some fight promoter is backing him against Sugar Ray Leonard." There were other such speculations flying around, but only the chief and his protégé really knew the details.

On the morning of the tournament, Basher was picked up at home by the chief's driver, who then called for the chief and they travelled south to the city where the battle was to take place that evening.

Following the dozen or so preliminaries, the MC announced the eagerly awaited match. Gloves were inspected and the combatants went to their respective corners. The chief, irritatingly digging his elbow constantly into the ribs of his counterpart, settled down to watch the destruction of that gentleman's champion. The bell was sounded and Basher came to his senses in the rear seat of the official car, his aching head resting on the lap of the chief!

For the remaining miles of the journey home there was a strained silence. Mutterings of apology from Basher fell on ears reluctant to listen, and it was with some relief that he staggered from the vehicle and into his house an hour or so later.

Of course the whole story came out the next day and the chief, being obliged to suffer the taunts of his former high ranking colleagues over the telephone, sent for Basher.

"I would not of minded if you had landed just one blow, instead of prancing round the ring like a ballet dancer," he complained."

Basher realised that it was time for an explanation and that he must put the chief in the picture before somebody else did. He confessed that he had never fought anyone in the whole of his life, either in or out of the ring.

"Then how do you account for your appearance," enquired the chief, raising his voice to a volume which could be detected in several offices along the corridor.

" Well, you see sir, when I was about six years old I tripped and my face hit the kerb. Terrible mess my mother said it was and ..."

"Get out, get out !" yelled the chief. We all knew the full facts in no time, but the public didn't, and Basher Molloy spent many more years on the beat, always successfully defusing volatile situations with his grim features.

There were of course plenty of officers with fighting reputations, which, if not supported by accompanying features like those of Basher, were well and truly supported by their powerful strength and ability to make good use of their fists. It was always a comfort to have that category of officer at your side when on Friday and Saturday nights from eleven until twelve thirty, the duties involved coupling up with the man on the adjacent beat. This method of working was designed to keep customers who had left the main road hostelries at closing time, from hanging about and consequently making a nuisance of themselves.

A downpour of rain at that time of night, was worth fifty patrolling coppers. On a warm dry Saturday, P.C. Kevin Clarke and I were working together when a young woman approached us and reported that a fight was in progress in one of the nearby pubs. She said that there was a wedding celebration and in the true tradition of the local community, a battle had ensued.

"You'll 'ave to watch out, they've all brought 'ammers with 'em," she warned. We pushed our way into the spacious assembly room, where indeed there was a fierce altercation taking place and our informant was right about the hammers as all of the male guests seemed to possess one. I disarmed one particularly irate individual as he raised his arm to swing the weapon at me and began to drag him toward the door. A large woman, who was screaming oaths, leapt onto my back in an effort to free my capture and I was obliged to bang her against the wall behind me several times until she abandoned her purpose.

Kevin, seeing my difficulty, began to clear the doorway by punching everyone within reach and soon the floor was covered with unconscious combatants. One roughneck, who had somehow survived one of Kevin's uppercuts, was brought outside in an arm lock of steel and the pair of us propelled our loudly critical prisoners to the station.

As the two were being charged, the double doors flew open and into the office burst two drunken women. The younger was wearing a heavily bloodstained wedding dress, whilst the older female was resplendent in a cheap pale blue suit ripped beyond repair. It transpired, that by coincidence, Kevin had arrested the bridegroom and I the best man, whilst the woman was the mother of the bride and it was she whom I had to batter against the wall in order to get her off my back. All four spent the night in the cells and were bailed on Sunday morning. On Monday they appeared at court and were fined forty shillings (£2) each.

Many of the main road pubs could be described as fighting houses and each sported its own champions, who were always willing to uphold both their personal reputation and that of their local. The Cherub's Arms boasted a host of champions; in fact it was the watering hole for thieves and prostitutes who daily and nightly, wandered the half mile from their impoverished homes which bounded that hostelry, to infest the city centre.

On a Sunday however, the centre was deserted and they could all be found spending the day, and their ill-gotten gains in the Cherub's Arms. On one of those Sundays, P.C. Mick Mulligan, stood on the pavement outside those very premises. He had been in the job for a mere two months and was still in the process of finding his way about. The dirty damp streets and run down housing were a long way from the beautiful meadows and rocky coast line of County Clare, but the farm was too small to maintain him and his older brother. Both had travelled to Dublin, where a recruiting campaign for the Manchester City Police had attracted him. His brother, having enquired into a similar situation, had gone to be a New York cop.

His daydreaming was brought to a halt by a crash of glass as a piece of heavy furniture left the pub via a window and he turned to stride into the place. Normally, an extra large man like Mick, especially in uniform, would have had some effect on an unruly mob, but not this lot. Around forty men were fighting with each other, all of whom were vastly experienced and as the officer attempted to call for order, a stray pint pot struck him full on the chest. He identified his assailant and lunged into the heaving mass towards him.

The hapless hooligan received a punch from Mick which sent him staggering backwards, taking half a dozen of the rioters down to the floor with him. Someone knocked the constable's helmet off and he lost his temper, felling everyone within reach and then smashing anyone else who came within range of his giant fists. Soon, any of them still able to move, had either escaped the culling by feigning death or had managed to hide in the landlord's private quarters.

Left with nobody else to destroy, Mike replaced his helmet and walked out of the premises. The training he had tried to assimilate in his first three months appeared not to cover the circumstances so he strolled away from the scene and continued to work his beat. There were many unofficial reports of the situation. Ancoats Hospital, for instance, listed a record number of patients who had fallen at home or tripped on uneven footpaths that Sunday, but non were related, though were consistent with, being on the receiving end of a copper's pile driver blows.

If the Chief Superintendent had the facts, which was most likely, he kept them to himself. Most senior officers in those days came up through the ranks and understood what working a beat entailed. As for Mike, he was the toast of the district and continued for years to be highly respected in the area.

Chapter Five

Harpurhey, a district on the B division, was my favourite area in which to work. Thousands of terraced houses occupied hundreds of small streets, with a shopping thoroughfare running through its middle. When most of its residents were tucked up for the night, there was, to some degree, a moment or two in which the men on their beats might relax their vigil, according to the individual's choice. These moments required some skill in their arrangement as a rendezvous point had to be

31

made every three quarters of an hour at a prearranged point, any of which may be where the sergeant had decided to turn up and woe betide any constable who was not at his point without a good reason.

At one o'clock in the morning, I turned from the shops into a side street and tried in vain to avoid the icy wind by keeping as close to the houses as I could. Earlier in the week there had been a heavy fall of snow, which quickly froze over and had remained in its slippery preserved condition making progress precariously slow. The heavy double breasted overcoat and cape failed to deflect the easterly wind, and the occasional deep doorway offered little comfort.

As I looked along the street I became aware of a figure dashing from one dim pool of gas light and emerging at another, before vanishing into an entry which passed along the rear of the houses to my right. I trotted as best I could to the end of the passage, where I met the apparition in full flight. In the darkness I saw that my quarry was completely naked and as I took hold of his arm it felt like a joint of frozen lamb. I pulled him under a gas lamp, where, to my surprise, between spasms of teeth chattering he said, "Woodie, it's me!"

He tried to adopt a foetus position, presumably in an attempt to limit the area of wind and I pulled him up from the pavement. I saw he was the officer from the next beat, which prompted me to wrap the poor man in my cape and to assist him to the section station a couple of hundred yards away. There, he explained that he had been visiting a woman of his acquaintance who had neglected to inform him of the existence of her husband and that a few moments prior to my sighting of him, a key was heard to operate the lock of her front door.

"It's 'im," the woman had cried, at which my colleague had bolted, leaving his uniform and everything else, lying on the floor of her lounge. Having obtained the address of his assignation, I advised him to hide himself in the yard toilet until I returned. As I neared the address he had furnished I tried to think how best to approach such a delicate matter and as I knocked on the door I decided to pretend I was looking for a desperate criminal who had attacked a policeman and stolen his clothes and that he had been seen entering that address.

The young girl who answered the door turned out to be the sister of the woman involved, who lived at the address and it was she who had been heard turning the lock on her return from a night out. The husband was working away on a long term project and had not been home for months. Both women and myself, found the episode highly amusing and they were still laughing when I left them, carrying the officers equipment.

The section station was in darkness when I entered, and the errant constable was still hiding. I brought him out and having piled his uniform in a back room, informed him that the woman's husband wouldn't hand his stuff over saying that he preferred to hand it all over to the inspector at the time of registering an official complaint in the morning. His reaction to the news surprised me, as I knew him to be as thick skinned as any rhinoceros.

"My missus is going to kill me and I'm bound to get the sack," he wailed. Seeing that he was genuinely upset and on the threshold of collapse I confessed and gave him all his gear, immediately after which, I slipped out of the station. From several yards away I could hear him saying what he thought of me and I was pleased at seven o'clock, when we were signing off duty, to find he was beginning to see the funny side of the affair.

There is, and always shall be, a deep and wide gulf between the uniformed branch and the C.I.D. It is not as though detectives are recruited from some source of excellence, they each have to spend at least two years walking, or in these days driving about, in apparel which immediately discloses that they belong to the police. My first realisation of the public's attitude towards the C.I.D. was nothing to do with the officer involved.

I was in a shop where the proprietor was reporting a burglary to me and I took the opportunity to snatch a quick smoke. I had my back towards the door and the person I was talking to took the cigarette from my mouth, threw it onto the floor and stepped on it. "Your boss is coming in," he hissed, and at that moment, Detective Constable Arthur Acroyd entered the premises.

Later, as I walked along with him I told him what had taken place. " You always get that," he informed me. "It makes no difference how many times we tell people that we are simply constables, or sergeants, out of uniform, they will not have it. To them you are an inspector or above and nothing will shake them from that view, I gave up years ago." He was using the C.I.D. car and I cadged a lift to the station.

"What about when you produce your identity card, can't they see your rank on that?" I enquired.

"No one ever examines them. As a matter of fact I lost mine a few years ago," he admitted.

"That's a hanging offence Arthur," I said.

"You're telling me," he said. " That's why I didn't dare to report it. I saw a card in a joke shop which had the same dimensions, laminated and all that, so I bought it and used it ever since," he explained, at the same time producing the document for my inspection.

The card was, as he said, the exact size of the official document, but the similarity ended there It bore the image of a fully made up clown, with red nose and large ears. There, in bold lettering, it advertised Blackpool Circus, with the name of the clown, Bippo, blazoned across it!

"Plenty of wise guys have demanded to see it," Arthur revealed. " But not one of them has noticed that it wasn't genuine, or at least if they did they didn't say anything."

I next met Detective Constable Acroyd, by surprise, at an incident which tended to verify the rift I have mentioned. There was an old first war army hut on the division which served as a police club. The frequenting of licensed premises when off duty was discouraged, and it was believed that such an establishment, where the men could imbibe, out of the gaze of the public was the answer. Of course, no effort had been made to present the premises as comfortable or pleasant to be in and apart from a few old chairs and tables, plus a battered tuneless piano, it could have reverted to its former use within fifteen minutes.

There was however an adequately stocked bar, from which the steward, an elderly one armed man, struggled to provide a service to be expected from a barman with a full complement of limbs. Despite all these shortcomings the hut was an ideal venue for the frequent celebrations which were held there. An officer's birthday, promotion or divorce, for instance, would usually be well supported and in the absence of any senior ranks, letting the hair down was practised on a large and boisterous scale.

I had received an invitation on the grapevine to give a send off to an officer who was retiring from the uniform branch and I arrived at the club on the appointed evening around eight o'clock. The entrance was in the centre of the hut, and as I walked in I noticed that the retirement guests were gathered at the end of the room, to my right. At the opposite end of the club were gathered a crowd of C.I.D. men.

As I was still serving as a uniformed officer at the time I naturally joined the appropriate camp. Within a short time the club became packed, apart from a narrow no man's land between the factions. The steward, by natural selection, endeavoured to serve beer to the best of his ability and keep both sections contented. It was obvious that there had been a double booking of events which had escaped the attention of the steward, each party having expected to enjoy an exclusive occupation of the club.

Of course, due to the intense animosity between the departments concerned, neither was aware of the other's plans. By chance, the piano was sited in the area occupied by the uniform lads and one of the group, an accomplished player, took up a position at the instrument and led us all in the loud execution of songs learnt during our various military campaigns. The first rendition made reference to the monarch of a middle eastern country and his spouse, whose sexual preferences were somewhat peculiar. There followed further selections of non political correctness, which tended to besmirch whole communities in foreign lands, at least those lands in which many of those present, including myself, had the misfortune to serve our country.

The din from all this was making it impossible for those at the other end of the room to converse and the situation was fast becoming intolerable. The detectives had engaged a comedian to entertain their party, who, after four attempts to carry out his engagement, demanded his fee and left. It all began to develop into the likelihood of fisticuffs and in view of the fighting capabilities of many present, at both ends of the room, some dampening down was urgently required. A high ranking C.I.D. officer who had been invited, solved the problem by persuading the detectives to pack up and transfer to a pub he knew which was outside the force area. After their departure, the uniform branch spread out across the room and carried on until closing time.

In the course of time petty restrictions as to where officers could spend their free time crumbled away and with them, the old army hut. The cultural gap however, grew ever wider, with neither side letting the other know what they were about, or the venue of any intended social event.

Some licensed premises on the divisions were more popular

with police officers than others and of those, some were the haunts of the uniform branch, whilst others were exclusively the watering holes of the C.I.D.

A few of the places were made use of by the uniformed sergeants and woe betide any constable who took it upon his self to encroach those hostelries without permission from those sergeants. There were, in contradiction, a handful of pubs or clubs to which all departments resorted, though the barriers of social intercourse were still firmly in place.

To regulate the licensing laws, each division maintained a department of half a dozen men, with a sergeant, known as the Plain Clothes Department. In addition to their duties in that direction they investigated some crimes, like indecent assaults , woundings etc. The sergeant and constables would complete a twelve month tour in the squad and then revert to uniform, so there would be a constant turn over of the staff.

The Lighthouse was one of the inns which fell into the category of a multi branch drinking facility, not least due to the friendly personality of the licensee. Maggie, an attractive middle aged widow, took over the licence following the death of her husband when both she and he were comparatively young and many officers felt it was their duty to comfort her over the years. In return she made it clear that the police in general would be ever welcome. Retirement and promotion celebrations were often held in the assembly room upstairs and if the occasions went on into the early hours of the morning, so be it.

Maggie's non police customers were also treated with common sense and when it came to gulping down their drinks at eleven, perhaps another hour would be allowed to consume her fine ale. The Plain Clothes Sergeant, having completed his year in office, was replaced by a sergeant who already held the title of Sergeant Killjoy and the talk throughout the division was one of gloom at his appointment.

He was well known for his sobriety and vociferous condemnation of policemen who accepted favours from publicans. Most of the other sergeants were jealous of the appointment, feeling that had they been selected they would made much better use of the undoubted power which the post would bring them. Amongst the rest, those delighted to have him removed from the post of Charge Office Sergeant for a year were prominent, not least the flotsam and jetsam who found themselves incarcerated for the night.

Killjoy was a novice musician and enthusiastic in that pastime. Practising the violin at home tended to create unpleasantness between him and his wife so that whenever he was on the night relief he practised in the remoteness of the cell corridor. The recitals which were scratched out during the early hours failed to impress the occupants of the cells, who, as a captive audience, were forced to endure the awful renderings, instead of enjoying an otherwise, though far from comfortable, night's slumber.

Many of those affected complained to the magistrates and described the situation as police cruelty, prompting their worships to dismiss the claims as ridiculous. It had been hinted to the newly appointed enforcer that The Lantern ought to be considered as his primary target and that he would be wise not to discuss his plans in that direction with anyone, including his own little department. He knew very well that there would be no chance of a successful raid on the premises should the slightest whisper get about of his intentions.

Within a few days he bumped into the Plain Clothes Sergeant of another division who he knew to be of the same mind as himself with regard to anyone enjoying themselves. His counterpart was asked to raid the offending pub on his behalf, under the auspices of their respective chief superintendents of course. The other sergeant was at first reluctant, as he had plenty to do on his own patch, but when he was told that the C.I.D. were the main offenders, he agreed. Late on the following Saturday evening he met the other sergeant and his men a few streets away from the target and there the die was cast. He had directed the members of his own squad to something trivial on the opposite side of the division in order that they would be well out of the way.

At eleven fifteen, he, the other sergeant and his team, marched into The Lighthouse to find it crowded with unsuspecting customers and Maggie pulling merrily away at the pumps.

"I am the Licensing Sergeant," bawled Killjoy above the noisy chatter. Maggie came from behind the bar and with a puzzled expression, said "I don't know you men."

"Never mind about that," shouted her adversary "These people are consuming alcohol after permitted hours and you are supplying it to them. You are all being summonsed for that."

The accompanying officers efficiently passed amongst the offending drinkers, gathering their names and addresses, threatening Michael Mouse and Bernard Montgomery with arrest unless they gave their correct particulars. In the course of time they had all the information which would be required by the court and bidding the trembling Maggie goodnight, they all trooped out of the place.

News of the raid broke the next day like that of some terrible catastrophe and internal telephone lines were alive with the swapping of details. At first, nobody could understand how it could have been done without anyone being aware of its imminence. The licensing team was made up of Maggie's friends, apart from Killjoy, and at most would have advised her to close on time for a week if matters had become serious.

Inquests held everywhere quickly revealed the truth and messages of sympathy were swiftly passed to Maggie. A representative group held a meeting away from the division and a plan to save the situation was hatched. A glance at the licensing laws reminded the committee that an exception to the offences being reported was capable of being employed.

" It says here, that intoxicating liquor may be consumed on the premises under special circumstances," read out one of the officers, from a copy of Stone's Manual he had smuggled out of the C.I.D. office. Most of those present had a vague notion of what he was referring to and asked him to read out the relevant passages.

"It says," began the officer, balancing the bulky volume on the shoulder of a colleague, "that the supply of intoxicating liquor on licensed premises to any private bona fide friends, entertained by him at his own expense, shall not constitute an offence."

There followed a pooling of suggestions as to how this loophole could be presented to the court, the culmination to which resulted in a brilliant, if precarious scheme. Tasks were allocated immediately to individuals and the meeting broke up. Perhaps the most difficult assignment went to the officer whose task it was to rehearse Maggie for her part. She was a woman of the world to say the least, but her experience of lawyers and their methods, when some poor soul stood trembling in the witness box, was not as wide as that of her benefactors.

"You will be saying, on the date of the hearing, that the date on which you were raided was in fact your wedding anniversary and that all those summoned for boozing after time were your bona fide friends and that they have attended your anniversary to celebrate in the same way for the past thirty odd years." explained the officer.

"But I've been a widow for the past twenty," said Maggie. "Never mind, you'll have to make a point of not mentioning that," said her harassed tutor.

After a great deal of persuasion and a graphic illustration of her predicament, should she fail to go along with it, she relented and agreed to everything. Cards bearing invitations to the celebrations, dated both for the date of the offence and for the same date in the previous year, were swiftly printed with the particulars of the offenders, captured on the night of the raid, boldly displayed. All the offenders were visited and brought into the plan, by men whom they believed were solicitors acting for Maggie and needless to say, all readily agreed to play the part.

A large cake was supplied, upon which was the legend. 'Happy Anniversary Maggie', the date being of the previous year. A photograph bearing all the customers involved, was produced showing them in the pub with that large piece of confectionery on a table before them.

All this evidence found its way to the right quarter and the matter was dropped. Sergeant Killjoy was reprimanded for not looking into the matter properly and returned to uniform. His replacement, following a traumatic experience while soldiering in Egypt some years before, was interested only in clearing the division of prostitutes, which left him no time to bother with licensed premises.

Chapter Six

The ancient long retired constable sitting at a lone table in the police club nodded at me over the rim of his empty glass.

"Fancy a pint George?" I called over to him from the bar. I took both his and my own glass over to him and took a seat at the table. " Ever tell you about Teddy Wick on the A Division?" he asked as he pretended to search franticly for his cigarettes."I 'ad 'em when I come in here," he grumbled. I placed my packet of fags down before him and invited him to help himself, which he did and drawing deeply on the deadly weed, leant back in his chair with the air of a man who had been finding enjoyment in the practise for the past sixty odd years.

"Aye, Teddy was one of those likeable scallywags wot the sergeants and inspectors considered to be a sort of challenge to 'em. They knew he spent most of his time boozing on duty, but try as they could, they weren't ever able to catch him. The trouble was that he was a hero, with no less than three medals for bravery. The first award was for rescuing a family from a blazing house, the second for arresting a madman who was shooting at shoppers and the last one for rescuing a tramp from a watery grave."

The storyteller took several loud swigs at his empty glass and when I came back from the bar with a refill, he continued. "That last medal was always spoken about in scathing terms and cruel allegations were made, out of his earshot of course, due to his violent temper and great strength. Most of the supervising officers were giving up hope of ever catching him out and felt that even if they were successful, his record of gallantry would get him off the hook. A newly promoted inspector came to the division and having been acquainted with old Wick's habits, determined to triumph.

"On one of them cold foggy nights in November, the inspector stalked his quarry with the expertise of his ancestors hunting deer in the Highlands. The constable made a sudden detour into a side street and when the hunter followed there was no sign of him. There was, however, a pub in the street and the inspector had no doubt that the officer was inside."

The old copper took another of my proffered cigarettes and slid his empty pot across the table. After the vessel had been recharged he fell to silence and I had to remind him where he was up to.

"Oh, that's right, he was in the Shamrock on Blossom Street," he recalled. "The landlord happened to glance out of the window and caught sight of the inspector who was crouching in a doorway opposite. He informed his guest, who hastily left by the back yard and set off at a trot towards the riverside where he was due to be at that time. The inspector, who had run in pursuit of the sound of the constable's footsteps, turned a corner which brought him to a low wall separating the footpath from the river. He stood very still and while 'e was fighting to get 'is breath back, fancied 'e heard a yell of terror. 'e leaned over the wall and through the mist 'e made out two figures, half in the water and half on the stone stairs wot lead up to the road. Anyway the beam from 'is torch lit up Wickie who was dragging someone else out of the river. The next few minutes were taken up by the inspector blowing 'is whistle for 'elp and 'im pumping water out of both bathers whilst the two beat men that turned up in answer, called for an ambulance."

The story teller took a brief respite, during which he explained that he would have liked to return my generosity, if only he could afford it. The crafty old rogue knew that he had me too keen to know the outcome to abandon him now and a freshly drawn pint of his favourite bitter caused the narrative to be continued.

"Immediately 'e was able to, 'e told the inspector 'is version of wot 'appened. 'e said that 'e was strolling along by the river when a loud cry of distress reached 'im and it was then that 'e saw a poor man struggling in the water, so 'e took 'is uniform off and plunged in after 'im. Wickie took a fortnight on the sick and whilst 'e was away, the rescued man, who turned out to be a local drunk, was questioned over and over, as to what had really happened that night, and all the time 'e kept giving the same answer.

"The incident was a blank to 'im, other than that 'e 'ad been sitting on the wall drinking from a bottle and the next thing being in the river 'olding on to a big copper. In the end there was nothing for it than for the inspector to report that the officer's account was absolutely true. Amongst the rest of us there was no doubt as to the truth and the grumbling about the medal went on for years afterwards. The seething inspector went on to high rank and was always unable to walk past the venue of the heroic rescue without tutting."

During next few years I found myself employing the same cunning of Constable Wick, a cunning which had to be developed by every officer, if he was to be any use to his police force and the law abiding folk who placed a reliance on him. Number fourteen beat covered a large area of the B Division and though it was thickly populated it was devoid of pubs, something to do with the fact that most of the houses and all of the land, belonged to the Deans and Cannons of Manchester, who had let off the area on the understanding that no licences to supply liquor were ever to be granted.

A hard and fast rule, to the effect that no officer should encroach on another's beat, except when necessary in the furtherance of duty, was always strictly observed, so that if you were anything other than a staunch teetotaller and you found yourself allocated to fourteen beat for the usual six weeks tour, it was a period of misery to say the least. I began my tour of that beat during a hot summer having moved on in the strict rotation of going round the division on the odd numbered beats, eighteen of them, then round again on the eighteen even numbered ones.

Some constables followed the routine quite happily for the whole of their service, resulting in a knowledge of the division and most of its inhabitants, past and present which could never be matched today.

Others, like myself, in an effort to get off the treadmill, committed themselves to hours of study in order to pass the difficult qualification for promotion examinations. The trouble with that was a pass did not mean a promotion.

On the second day of my period on the dreaded beat I saw a furniture van being unloaded into one of those tiny corner shops much in evidence in that time. These convenient outlets were open early and closed late, selling everything from safety pins to cigarettes and beer. I made myself known to the incoming proprietor, who asked me inside and invited me to help him in ascertaining whether a keg of beer, left by his predecessor was still palatable. It turned out to be very much so and between us we prevented the contents from ever becoming sour.

It was the beginning of a long friendship with Tommy, as he was named, insisting that I called in whenever I was passing. Towards the end of the six weeks one of the inspectors visited me and as we strolled through the darkened streets he touched on the subject of fourteen beat being unpopular.

"It's got no pubs on it you know," he smirked. He was known to everyone as Uriah Heep, due to his habit of constantly wringing his bony hands in an ever so 'umble attitude and if you should want the Superintendent to know anything, you had merely to tell Uriah, in confidence of course.

"No doubt you can't wait to move over onto sixteen beat next week," he said wringing his hands in anticipation of my reply.

"Well, sir, it's a rotten beat all right and these last weeks have seemed like years," I lied.

Needless to say, I was not moved on, as would have been the case under normal circumstances, but instead was kept on the erstwhile punishment beat for a further twelve lovely weeks, keeping my pal Tommy company at every opportunity. Always, after I related what had taken place between the inspector and me, Tommy referred to me as Brer Rabbit.

"Why do you call me that Tommy?" I asked.

" Have you never read those Uncle Remus tales where Brer Rabbit got caught by the fox? He begged the fox to eat him if he wished, but pleaded not to be thrown into the briar patch as he hated it. The fox, wishing him to suffer as much as possible, threw Brer Rabbit right into the centre of the briars, only to see the rabbit dancing with glee amongst the thorny bushes he had spent most of his life in," said Tommy.

" Do you see what I mean?" he asked.

" Think so," I replied.

Some very desirable posts were in existence and seemed to have been filled by individuals for many years, it being as though they were permanent fixtures and didn't actually belong to the police service, although of course they did. The extensive fruit and vegetable market in the city centre was regulated by a staff of policemen, headed by a chief inspector. All the officers were members of the police band and therefore only worked on day shifts. The chief inspector, though not one of the musicians, had been in charge of the market for as long as anyone could recall.

At long last, after sticking it out until the age of sixty, he was to retire on Christmas Day. As fate will often have it, he developed pneumonia just three weeks before his last day of duty and the prospect of visiting all the stallholders, as he had always done on a Christmas Eve, seemed to be as doomed as himself.

Between bouts of delirium, he confided with his wife as to the likelihood of attending the market in order to gather the many gifts showered on him each yuletide, especially on this, his last Christmas with them. There was much talk in the neighbourhood with regard to his illness and the frequent visits of the doctor to his home. One of the locals, who made it her duty to collect door to door for a wreath whenever a neighbour passed on, had already begun her rounds.

On the morning of Christmas Eve, immediate neighbours were astonished to see the chief inspector being assisted on a wobbly walk, in full uniform, though wrapped in a blanket, down his path to a taxi, in which he was transported to the market. Somehow he managed to visit every stallholder, propped up most of the time by his devoted spouse and the cab driver, grumbling about the weight of the gifts to be carried, delivered all and sundry to the address he had brought the invalid from some time earlier.

The coughing, wheezing, barely alive chief inspector was eventually put back to bed and his doctor once again summoned to his side. Of course there was no mention of his trip to town and twenty four hour nursing was the recommendation of the physician. The officer eventually recovered from his illness and the last date of his service having arrived during his absence from the job, he never again set foot on the market.

His long suffering wife strove to make use of the large stock of fruit and vegetables which were stacked in every room of the house and in the absence of any spark of generosity on the part of her husband, was obliged to refrain from any thoughts of passing any of it to neighbours or relatives.

Soon, without the modern day domestic freezing facilities, the commodities rotted away and just a few weeks into the new year, they no longer existed. The neighbour who had been collecting for a wreath, gave the money back to the donors, only to recommence the procedure a week before the following Christmas when the former chief inspector went to that great fruit and vegetable market in the sky!

I hated to be given duties which confined me to the four walls of the police station, preferring always to be in the open air and enjoying the comparative freedom of working on my own, so that when I was directed to replace the Charge Office Clerk during his two weeks summer leave it was a source of annoyance to me. However as I had recently passed the promotion to sergeant examinations, such duties were considered to be of value whenever a promotion was up for selection.

On my first night in the office, a busy Friday, with prisoners being pushed up against the counter every few minutes, the sergeant and I had barely a minute to relax. If either of us knew that in later years the situation would be talked of as stressful, it would have been easier to understand why we constantly lost our temper with both the officers and their arrestees and why, when things calmed down in the early hours, the sergeant would settle down to forty winks.

As instructed, I woke him at five am as it was time to bail out most of the overnight guests and hand their property, taken from them earlier back to them. I passed the keys of the safe over to the sergeant, who took out the individual property bags which I in turn emptied out on to the counter. Each of the men being bailed picked up the items concerned, signed for them and left the building, in the surety that he would appear at court later in the day.

When the morning shift came on, pleasantries were exchanged between us and the sergeant and I went home to bed. The morning sergeant, requiring the keys to the safe, in order that the property of those prisoners being woken up for transportation to court might be handed to the driver of the vehicle taking them there, was unable to locate them. Just as I was about to collapse into a deep sleep I was turned out to return to the station where I was asked about the keys.

I felt convinced that I had seen the night sergeant with them after I had opened the safe and so he also was sent for. Much debate and clever reconstruction was carried out which got everybody nowhere and the morning sergeant declared that he could not delay reporting the loss a moment longer. It was a decision which momentarily cleared my weary head into remembering that the safe keys were on the counter when the men being bailed were picking up their personal belongings.

All present concluded that the offending keys had been inadvertently picked up by one of those men, who must still have them in his possession. By then the afternoon shift had begun to arrive for duty and the incoming sergeant, having been appraised of the situation, reluctantly agreed to postpone reporting the loss to the Divisional Chief Superintendent, so long as somebody made the necessary urgent enquiries at the addresses of the men they had bailed.

By a process of elimination and well into the afternoon, the finger pointed to a young Irishman who, his landlady declared, had arrived at his digs earlier and told her he was fed up with being locked up every time he had a glass of beer and had left to catch the boat home to The Republic Of Ireland.

His address in Endenderry was obtained and a telephone message to the Garda in that town was despatched immediately. Inspector O'Toole was informed of the circumstances, slightly embellished with an account of the keys being an exhibit in a murder case. It was well known that the police in Ireland were always helpful in such matters and when the inspector promised to trace our man we all grew a little more confidant.

The chief superintendent would very soon be carrying out one of his frequent inspections and as he always made a point of looking into the contents of the safe, therefore there were factions who were beginning to insist he be informed in the very near future. As if by some miracle a call was received from Inspector O'Toole just as the decision was made to report the matter.

"I found your man here now," said the inspector. "He found the keys in his pocket just as the train was getting into to town here and he says that as he didn't know where they'd come from he threw them out of the window of the train."

A loud groan came from the sergeant who was answering the call and everyone's spirits dropped to the cellar and beyond.

"I took him back up the line and we found them in a field. I've posted them to you," said the inspector.

After profuse terms of thanks were addressed to the Irish saviour of most of the B Divisional office staff, the recipient of the call announced the splendid result. The wanton keys arrived the very next day and took up their rightful place on the keyboard, never to leave home again. Everyone was happy, none more than myself, as I was banned from office duties for many years.

Chapter Seven

I walked into the C.I.D. office one Saturday and was collared immediately by the detective inspector.

"Have you got anything on today?" he asked.

"Nothing pressing," I replied.

"Then get off home and pack your razor, you're off to Dublin with Sergeant Raddle, to bring back a prisoner," he said.

A couple of hours later, the sergeant and I were rolling around on the Irish Sea in a non too stable ferry boat. The miscreant we were to bring back, was waiting for us at Mountjoy Prison, having served a two year sentence for crimes in the Republic and was now to be charged at Manchester with burglaries committed there before fleeing across the sea.

We were met at the dock by a detective from the Garda and transported by him to an address used frequently by officers on similar missions from Britain. The owner of the property served us breakfast and lost no time in telling us he was a sympathiser of the Irish Cause. Between fetching the toast and showing us to our rooms, he blamed the ancestors of both myself and the sergeant for the many unfortunate incidents which had apparently taken place over hundreds of years and I felt like jamming a chair behind the door handle whilst making use of the bathroom.

The prisoner could not be collected until Monday afternoon, which left the Sabbath to ourselves, or so we thought. The detective who had collected us from the boat and his colleague, came to the house within the hour. We had been warned that the Irish Police had a reputation for hospitality, believing that if visitors, such as ourselves, returned to our force and complained of not being legless during their stay, it would be a catastrophic disgrace.

Our hosts first drove us some miles into the countryside, having explained that the pubs were only permitted to serve bona fide travellers on a Sunday, and that an unfamiliar vehicle denoted bona fide travellers. We were more than glad to quit the unmarked police car as it constantly shaved the hawthorn hedges of the narrow lanes at speeds which were well outside the prescribed limit.

Inside the cosy little pub, we accepted the generosity shown to us and drank deeply the traditional ales of that fair isle. Later in the evening we were whisked at an even faster pace to Dublin Airport, where the Sunday rules didn't apply. Sometime in the early hours of Monday, I heard myself rambling incoherently to our hosts and noticing that my companion was sitting on the floor, fast asleep, I indicated that it was past our bedtime. We were driven to our lodgings and this time the erratic driving was of no particular concern to me. After a partly eaten breakfast, I signed a paper on behalf of the Queen, in which the six counties of Ulster were to be returned to the householder at our digs and steeled myself for another nightmare journey as we tore off to Mountjoy Prison.

The prisoner was not ready for collection until later in the day and we were obliged to be introduced to half a dozen licensees in the capital by our detective friends. Through a bleary haze, my companion fastened the handcuffs, we had remembered to bring, to the left wrist of our charge and to the right wrist of himself. At last we were safe in the cabin which had been specially allocated to us and I, stretching out onto my bunk, fell into a fitful sleep. I woke to hear from the ship's engines that we were out to sea and glancing around the empty cabin, was horrified to see the handcuffs, equally empty and dangling from the metal frame of the sergeant's bunk.

My first thought was that the prisoner had overcome the sergeant, taken the key and jumped over the side. Perhaps the sergeant had leapt in after him, a scenario which would leave me a lot of explaining to do. I staggered out of the cabin and half adjusting my feet to the pitching of the vessel, began a tour of the deck. In one of the bars I found the sergeant and the prisoner, enjoying bottles of stout together and at once, joined them. At six in the morning we arrived at Liverpool, entrained for Manchester where we handed the lad over at Bootle Street Police Station.

Before we parted, he shook our hands and thanked us for the best night out he had experienced for a couple of years. Then, I think, any night out would have been his best over that period.

I was in and out of the C.I.D. and other non uniform duties quite a lot which afforded me a great deal of valuable experience, sometimes baffling, as for instance the promotion of individuals whom you would have thought not fit to command a group of brownies, let alone hard bitten coppers. One such person, who had served as a major during the war, had joined the division and was pursuing an inactive career as a beat constable, when he was selected to join nine other constables who were to meet a visiting Inspector Of Constabulary at the Divisional Headquarters.

The ten were drawn up in the yard and the important visitor cast his eagle eye over them.

"What is that medal ribbon you are wearing?" enquired the inspecting dignitary, pointing to one at the end of four displayed on the major's tunic.

"That sir is the Military Cross," explained its bearer.

"That means you held a commission," he said. " What rank were you?" asked the Inspector Of Constabulary.

"A major sir" was the reply, executed in a cut glass accent which he had adopted after listening to former public schoolboys in the officer's mess. The inspection completed, the inspecting officer strolled away with the Chief Constable.

"Why is that man not in the C.I.D.?" he enquired of the chief, and the chief who knew nothing about him, said that he had plans for the major's transfer in the near future. Just in case the Inspector Of Constabulary took it upon himself to check up on his return to London, the major was transferred the next morning.

There was a full complement of detectives on the division and it was decided, at the highest level, to find a spot for him in the newly formed Aliens Department in police headquarters downtown. He turned up for duty the following day wearing the C.I.D. uniform of trilby hat and light brown raincoat. The staff at the Aliens Branch, was a sergeant and two constables, all of whom had been there for several months and their duties involved the regulation of the growing numbers of foreigners arriving in the city having been displaced at the end of the war.

The fact that no one in the office spoke any language other than English made the job extremely difficult. There were a few officers pounding beats who were fluent in one or other European tongue, but the powers that be preferred to leave them there. One of the daunting tasks performed by the staff, was to examine those newspapers which were considered to be subversive and the detective who passed the news-stand on the corner of St. Ann's Square every morning, picked up the National Irishman and the Daily Worker, in order that the sergeant might cut out anything that required to be shown to the chief.

When it was discovered that the major would be passing the stand, he was instructed to carry out that duty and was given the fund from the petty cash.

"Do you mean to say the fellow just hands the papers over?" asked the new boy incredulously. The sergeant, a man well renowned for his jokes said, "Of course not, you have to give the code word, it's 'black puddings'."

The following morning when the major entered the office he did not have the newspapers with him and in answer to the sergeant's query he explained that he had approached the news vendor and whispered the code word in his ear.

"The fool walked away from me and stood at the other end of the stall. Then, of course, I realised that someone must be watching us, so I said 'good morning' to him and left," said the errand boy. The major stayed in that department for many more years and retired with the rank of superintendent.

Of course, to pretend that we were all perfect and never made a mistake, would be to tempt fate, and most such errors of judgement were made in good faith, as of that of a good friend who belonged to that weird band of men, the road patrol division.

Fresh sections of the new motorways were rapidly appearing and the police were having to learn how to deal with a new menace, the super speeders.

"I honestly believe that when a motorist gets onto the motorway, he is so scared that he drives like a madman in order to get the ordeal over with as quickly as possible," observed my friend, whilst showing off the new Land Rover so recently allocated to him. These road patrol officers lived and breathed their job and their senior officers held sway over them by merely hinting that should they put a single foot wrong, they would be put back onto foot patrol.

Alec, as my friend was called, had been posted to a new road patrol depot at the Birch Services on the M62. His beat, as it were, was between the depot and the boundary, where the motorway continued into the care of The Lancashire Constabulary and at two o'clock on a freezing January morning, he left the cosiness of the depot canteen, where he had taken his supper and trudged across the yard to his beloved police Land Rover.

It had begun to snow heavily during his absence and as he turned onto the road he praised the fact that he was in a four wheeled drive. He headed northwards, the heating system laboriously battling with the snow piling up on the windscreen and for several miles, his was the sole vehicle making use of the new road. A couple of hundred yards from his turning back point, he was surprised to see a motorcycle on the hard shoulder, its rider standing a few feet away from it. Alec pulled in behind the bike and got out, immediately experiencing the force of the blizzard which had increased in severity whilst he had been driving.

The biker, helmeted and resembling the Michelin Man, with a bulky scarf wrapped around the mouth and nose, was trying to say something, but the words were snatched by the fierce wind and carried away across the moors. His own queries were likewise wasted on the blizzard and both resorted to a kind of sign language.

At length, Alec, wishing he had brought his overcoat out with him, diagnosed a frozen carburettor and after several teeth chattering attempts to convey that intelligence, decided to employ a method of de-freezing it, well known to motor cycle enthusiasts the world over. As he undid his trousers it seemed to him that the howling wind had become even icier and that it was directing itself almost exclusively to his nether regions and it was only thanks to the pint of tea he had consumed earlier that he was able to begin the treatment at all. At first there appeared to be no response to his efforts, then, a trickle followed by a gushing flow, directed with great effort onto the carburettor, creating a satisfying cloud of steam, at the termination of which he stood back and motioned to the motorcyclist that the machine would now start.

The biker, gave a wave of appreciation, waddled onto the bike and shot off across the boundary. Back in the police vehicle he shivered for a while and as it warmed up he began to congratulate himself on a successful night's work. It then struck him that he had not bothered to check any particulars and that he may have assisted someone who had in fact stolen the bike. He decided that the whole thing would be best forgotten and he signed off duty at seven o'clock without mentioning it to a soul.

About ten days after the episode, the sergeant at the depot called Alec aside. "There's a letter here that was sent to the boss and judging from the time and date of the incident I believe it was you the writer is talking about," said the sergeant.

Alec knew it must be to do with the biking occurrence and with a feeling of impending discipline and the return to foot patrols, he read.

'Dear Chief Constable.

At 1-0a.m. on the 10th of January, my motorbike broke down on the M62 and I thought I would be frozen to death, then one of your constables arrived in a police vehicle. He eventually got my bike to start by a unique method I had never witnessed before. I was intrigued to say the least and the officer has every right to be pleased with himself.

Yours faithfully
Agatha Louise Green.'

About the same time as the motorbike incident, I was on leave and had gratefully accepted an invitation from an old army friend who lived in a quiet picturesque hamlet in Shropshire, to stay with him and his family for a few days. My pal met me at the station then broke the short journey to his home by persuading me to join him in a glass of beer. His local, an old coaching inn, looked as though some Hollywood film designer had built it for some film about England in the middle ages. The thatched roof and the welcome interior were far removed from the impersonal drinking dens of my own town.

The licensee was wearing a bandage which had been wrapped around his head very professionally by someone and the conversation amongst those around the bar, centred on the reason for the ministration of what was apparently, a nasty wound. I gathered that late the previous evening, two young lads had entered the premises and had to be warned by the landlord with regard to their foul language. One of them, a big ginger haired lout with a Liverpool accent, picked up a soda siphon and brought it down on the head of the licensee, whilst his companion held back any would be rescuers.

" Good job Doctor Green was in," said the landlord's wife as she came in from the kitchen. "He stopped it bleeding and when I got the bandage from the first aid box, he dressed Joe's head straight away." I asked whether the police had been informed and a customer said that he had put a note through Albert's letter box that morning.

"Albert's the Village Bobby," said my friend. "You have to understand that things are never rushed around here. He'll call in the pub this lunchtime, no doubt about that." He was right and within a quarter of an hour, the impressive figure of Albert, stooping to avoid smashing his head on the frame of the saloon bar door, stepped into the room.

"I found a note through the station door, something about ... blimey Norman, what's happened?" the constable enquired from the landlord. Everyone began to talk at once and after a few minutes the constable raised his arms and called for a bit of order.

"I guarantee it's them lot from the new road construction," concluded the officer, giving me the impression, that as far as he was concerned, that was that. He took his pint into a corner of the bar and began the laborious business of filling a pipe, which I learned some time later, had been in his family for at least two generations. My friend and I joined him at the table where I was introduced and it was revealed that I too was of the cloth.

I discussed the possibility of tracing the miscreants and went so far as to offer my assistance in the matter, though it was

Above: The old Rovers Return Inn, Shudehill, for centuries one of the city's best known landmarks, while below is the former Exchange railway station and Cromwell statue, also a well known site. The statue was later moved to Wythenshawe Park in south Manchester, where it remains to this day.

Manchester Coroner's Court

Manchester Magistrates' Court

An early street telephone box in Manchester, for use by the public

Vehicle check

Willert Street Police Station, Manchester

Piccadilly, Manchester, as it looked when the author walked the city centre beat

A Manchester city centre street

A prisoner in the cell block of an early 20th century Manchester police station

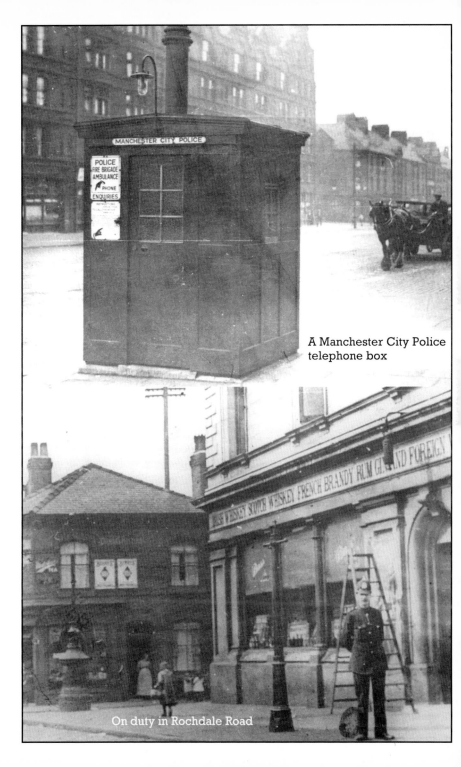

A Manchester City Police telephone box

On duty in Rochdale Road

The author pictured in various poses during his police career

quite apparent that he intended to do nothing, in the hope that the lads didn't return to the scene of the crime. After a few more drinks he seemed to fancy the idea of at least interviewing the persons concerned and he went home in order to don his uniform. Walking with Albert for a half hour made me realise that he had been denied the experience of rough and tumble police work on the streets of a big city and that it was not his fault that the most serious thing he had been asked to deal with in all his twenty odd years, was the incident on the previous evening.

We turned the corner of the lane and there before us lay a group of huts, the temporary homes of those employed in the construction of the new road.

"What happens is, every weekend the married ones go home to Liverpool and the single buggers stop on here," said Albert, with an air of one who can't be kidded.

I could see that on only one of the huts was the tiny chimney smoking and made directly to its door, it was unlocked and we entered. There were a series of beds along each side of the unkempt room, upon two of which lay the youths described. I got them to their feet and we hauled them off to Albert's humble house-come police station where, making use of a couple of sets of rusting handcuffs, I fastened the lads to a radiator.

I showed the officer how to obtain written confessions from them, then sent him to the pub to take witness statements from the doctor and several other persons who had been present during the wounding. At home, I would never have found anyone eager to go to court in such a matter and very often the attacker could not be prosecuted, as a reluctance to assist the police in any way at all, took preference as to whether a violent offender was punished within the law.

Whilst Albert was at the inn, I asked the Liverpool police to verify the addresses of the prisoners, who were apparently well known to them, and turned them loose, after telling them they would be summoned to court for their offences. When Albert returned I informed him what I had done and I showed him how to put the whole thing together, told him to send it in to his boss at Shrewsbury and not to mention my part in the affair.

I enjoyed the remainder of my short holiday and when I had been back in Manchester a month or two I received a letter from my old army pal. In it he said that Albert had been sent for by the Chief Superintendent who had congratulated him on his superb presentation and overall handling of a difficult case. He was asked if he would like to be transferred to the C.I.D., an offer he declined. A very sensible decision, I would have thought.

Shortly after that welcome break I returned to find that the newly opened, Manchester Crown Courts, were up and running and that I had become one of the thirty or so officers, chosen to work there. The hours were nine to five, which are heaven to someone who has worked on a shift basis for most of their life, plus the duties were little more than to make sure that the judges were protected from the wrath of anyone they had passed sentence on.

For the first few months I was required merely to sit in the public gallery of court number one and to chuck out anybody bent on misbehaviour. Many of the spectators were well known to my colleagues and myself and in consequence, they failed to get a chance for any naughtiness as we banned them from the gallery on sight. A sort of sideways promotion came my way after my stint on the public gallery, when the Court Inspector installed me in the public area of The Divorce Court.

This duty, though away from the skulduggery of the criminal trials, was dull and boring in the extreme. All day long, a policewoman and myself sat on a bench at the back of the small courtroom, forced to listen to the dreary domestic arguments which had culminated in the couples' appearances before an equally bored judge.

Their legal representatives presented the same scripts to these unfortunates, such as, "Did you on the tenth of June last year call your wife an old cow?" and so on.

Having endured these exchanges over a period, I was pleasantly surprised one Monday morning, when a newly introduced case began. I sensed that it was to be of a higher quality than normal when my policewoman associate whispered:

"Take a look at the husband, and look at the wife."

I saw a small middle aged man, who obviously didn't believe in squandering his money on clothes and then I looked at the plaintiff in the case about to be opened. She was tall, immaculately turned out, much younger than her husband with the air of a woman determined to get her own way.

"They've only been married for a few months," said the policewoman. "He's the landlord of a big pub and last year, when his mother died, the brewery told him he would have to leave as there was a new policy of their tenants having to be married couples."

I had been delayed in my arrival in the courtroom and was grateful to her for the information. The hapless hubby entered the witness box and took the oath in a nervous, almost inaudible voice and his wife's representative rose to attack him. Sentence by sentence the story unfolded, beginning with the sad death of his protector, who had held the licence for fourteen years following the demise of her husband. The premises were extensive, Edwardian in origin, and famous throughout Lancashire as a Mecca for those having an interest in bowling, particularly, the important national competitions held throughout the summer months.

The interior was on a grand scale and a wide stair case led directly from the main lobby and bars, to a balcony and a set of double doors to the private quarters. As I listened to the step by step descriptions, I failed to see what importance they could be to the tribunal and prepared myself for yet another boring day.

"When you were informed by the brewery of the terms they had introduced, with regard to your continuing to stay on, what was your reaction?" asked the plaintiff's barrister.

"I told them I would be wed within a few weeks," was the shaky reply of the respondent.

The case began to be of interest to me and I had a feeling it would turn out to be less of bore than I had first anticipated. My colleague appeared to have postponed her usual daydreaming and was listening intently. Questions, expertly put, and the required answers, began to reveal each detailed event as the full story gradually unfolded. He had decided that if he had to marry, it might as well be to someone pleasing to the eye and he began to survey the many barmaids in his employ. Somehow, word of the brewery's requirement had become common knowledge and the plainer of the girls began to take a lot more pride in their appearance. They need not have bothered, as the prospective husband and his money had already been earmarked by the woman now sitting in court. There had, it transpired, been a brief period of what may have been loosely termed, courtship and the nuptials were completed, with a minimum of celebration.

The new wife immediately seized control of both the bars and her erstwhile colleagues, making it impossible for them to implement their incomes in the time honoured practise of fiddling as they had previously enjoyed with impunity. Gossip in the pub and in the immediate locality, had it that the bridegroom was not claiming his conjugal rights, and that he was, in fact, one of the few men in town that had not had sexual contact with his bride over several years.

When he became aware of what was being banded about, he was furious and determined to prove the gossip ill-founded.

"Tell us what you did on Sunday the first of June at one o'clock in the afternoon, when the public bars were crowded with customers, many of whom were there to enjoy the bowling competitions which were taking place." said the examining counsel.

I could feel the atmosphere of interest which prevailed as those members of the public, in court began to sit up and take notice.

I had taken a bath and my wife was just leaving the shower, when I grasped her around her waist."

"You were both naked I assume?" said the advocate.

"That is correct," said the husband, avoiding the stares of his wayward wife. "I lifted her off her feet and she wrapped her legs behind my back, I think, in order to support herself,"

"What did you do at that stage ?" asked the barrister.

The husband fell silent and on prompting by the judge, he unfolded the scene. He told how he had turned, his naked spouse still clinging to her equally bare husband and walked through the double doors, onto the balcony, and in full view of all assembled in the lobby and bars, he called, "Now what have you to say about me not seeing to her properly?"

As I pictured the scene I inwardly chortled. There were audible sniggers in the room and I was able to avoid laughing aloud, until the policewoman grasped the sleeve of my tunic as she battled franticly to suppress a fit of hysterics. Her body was jerking convulsively which broke down my own efforts to contain myself and I entered into an uncontrollable bout of laughter.

Efforts to get out of the courtroom were impeded by the unreasonable clutching of my arm on the part of my colleague, until at last I was able to break free and stagger out into the great hall. There, my peals of laughter were amplified by the perfect acoustics of the building, attracting the attention of numerous barristers and their clients, not to mention witnesses and police officers. I was too weak to get to my feet and still screeching with mirth, someone pulled me along the hall to the toilets. I jammed my handkerchief into my mouth and sat in a cubicle battling to obliterate the image of the couple as they appeared on that balcony.

It was a long time before I was able to leave the sanctuary of those toilets and when I did I made my way to the police office of the court. There the inspector greeted me.

"The Divorce Court Judge has seen me and has asked that you and the policewoman are not assigned to his court in the future. Therefore, go back to your division," he said.

The next day I was on a beat, the brief spell of normal hours gone, not to return for many more years. I was in the city centre and off duty a few months after the incident, when I saw an officer who had worked at the court during the same period as myself. He was patrolling in St. Ann's Square and I asked why he was not at the courts.

"I had a similar problem as you," he said, mournfully.

"I was in the number one court gallery and during the lunch break I had a couple of pints. When I got back, I settled in the seat at the back of the gallery and suddenly I was aware of someone slapping my face. It turned out to be the Court Inspector and Sergeant. Apparently I'd dozed off and my snoring was so bad that the judge had to adjourn the case until they woke me up, which they said took all of twenty minutes." I didn't feel so badly done to after that.

Chapter Eight

To have to leave a family party in order to be on the night shift is bad enough, but when the celebrations are on a New Year's Eve it leaves a feeling of bitter resentment. Such was my attitude as 1961 moved over to allow the birth of 1962.

From walking out of Walter Street Station at 11pm, until well after the chimes of Manchester town hall clock had announced a fresh year, I must, one way or another, have seriously spoiled the alcohol fuelled celebrations of at least twenty revellers, six of whom let in the New Year locked in a cell.

When, around three in the morning, things began to quieten down, I spotted the man who was on the next beat to my own and went over to him. He was an old friend and had served in my own regiment as a piper. Much nostalgia passed between us and as we reminisced. I noticed a small elderly man, wearing a kilt and carrying a set of bagpipes walking towards us. He greeted us and my colleague asked to see the instrument. I explained that Jock was an excellent piper and the owner of the pipes handed them over to him.

"I come doon frae Dumfries every Hogmanay, booked to play at one of the hotels in the toon here," was the explanation of our new found friend.

Jock, the bag inflated beneath his arm, began the necessary tuning and went on to play an old favourite of mine and our regimental slow march, 'The Garb Of Old Gaul'.

The beautiful tones, though not appreciated by everyone, wailed out along the main road and I persuaded Jock to march with me into the back streets, where he changed to the quicker tunes, of 'Highland Laddie' and 'Scotland The Brave'. The residents of those tightly packed terraced houses, sleeping off their over indulgence, couldn't fail to hear the skirling as it bounced off the houses on both sides and screeched along the back entries. Bedroom lights were being switched on and as we turned back onto the main thoroughfare to the stirring rendering of 'The Black Bear', raised voices could be heard somewhere behind us.

The pipes were returned to their rightful owner who, on our advice, scurried off into the distance whilst Jock and I parted company, resuming our beats. At seven o'clock in the morning the night shift came into Walter Street Station in order to be signed off..

"Did any of you hear some bastard playing bagpipes at three this morning?" asked the Night Inspector. Met with an absence of reaction he flew into a rage.

"Don't tell me you couldn't hear it. I could and I was on the other side of the division. People have been ringing in all morning and asking why we haven't done anything about it."

I felt obliged to say something as the poor man had taken on a crimson hue, an indication, sometimes, that a heart attack was imminent.

"Well sir, there is the old legend," I began.

"What legend?" he bawled.

"The one about Bonnie Prince Charlie coming to Manchester in 1745. Apparently he entered the city from round here, his personal piper playing him in. His ghost and the piper have often been seen and heard by non believers on a New Years Day, and some say ..."

"Get out of my sight, the bloody lot of you. Get off home," the inspector yelled, as he disappeared into his office.

There were a number of men who never worked nights; instead they were employed on the morning shifts, not on a beat but on a set patrol. They were members of the Police Band and more often than not they were away from the divisions, either performing at some function, or more conveniently, at band practice..

These arrangements meant that the sergeants hardly bothered them, in that they couldn't be given a protracted duty or task, as they may called away to a band commitment at a moment's notice. Consequently those officers more or less, were without supervision and left to their own devices.

One of the bandsmen was Jimmy Manx, a likeable fellow and a life long committed bachelor. He was of course tall, with a handsome roguish face and a personality which appeared to drive women crazy with desire. One lady, though married, kept a photograph of Jimmy on the wall over her bed, and it had hung there throughout two of her previous marriages and the current one. What her explanation was must have been found satisfactory to the husbands as it remained there until her death many years later.

In the early nineteen-sixties, when Constable Manx was about forty, I met him in a favourite watering hole just off the division. He was in the company of a well known artiste, his current lady friend and I was introduced to her. I had recognised her as the female half of a singing duo who were supposed to be members of the Royal Family of one of those Scandinavian countries, the other half, to whom she was happily married, was not present. As the elegant blonde singer licked away at Jimmy's right ear, he asked her to make a telephone call on his behalf.

He explained that he had a friend, a licensee in the city, whose wife was insanely jealous and that he knew he would not be at his pub, as tonight being a Wednesday, was his evening off. He furnished his amorous companion with the telephone number and knowing that his friend's wife would be the one who would answer, instructed her as to the message.

"Hello," purred the husky voice of the Viking beauty. "I would like to speak to Vincent."

"Who's that?" asked the wife.

"Never mind, tell him that I have been waiting here for an hour. He promised to meet me at eight and take me for a meal and I'm going home."

The phone went dead and the fuming wife of the wayward Vincent sat down to prepare her opening salvo on his return. A couple of weeks after the practical joke, Jimmy was in uniform and at one in the afternoon was patrolling a stretch of the main road which passed through the division on its way to Rochdale, when a car drew to the kerb and the driver hailed him by name. The officer recognised the driver to be his old pal, Vincent.

"Get in Jim," he called, opening the passenger door. A quick glance up and down the road and Jimmy was sitting comfortably as the car sped off from the kerb.

"I'm just going to see another landlord then I'll bring you back and when you've signed off we'll go for a pint," said Vincent.

"Well I'm off at three," said Jimmy, as he pushed his helmet under the seat.

The conversation was that of various events which had taken place since last the pair had met, but the telephone call never came up and at long last, having turned from the road and onto a winding lane, which was little more than a cow path, they arrived at the top of the moorland and stopped on the dusty piece of ground serving as a car park at a little isolated inn.

"Come on in with me, there's a little snug you can wait in while I have a word with the landlord, then we can get back in time to sign off," said Vincent.

Jimmy, feeling a little uncomfortable, slipped into the tiny snug and entertained himself by admiring the rolling hills and trying to imagine the scene when his friend had returned to face the music after his little joke. Something like fifteen minutes went slowly by and he became restless. The premises were eerily quiet and he decided to remind Vincent of the need to get back.

He adjusted his helmet and stepped into the cramped bar, banging on the counter to attract attention. A beaded curtain which separated the public side from the private quarters was slowly drawn aside and the terrified countenance of a little old lady gingerly appeared. It was apparent that in the whole history of that ancient inn, the spectacle before her was a first time event.

"What's wrong constable?" she asked in a voice filled with a mixture of emotions, some of which, even she was unable to identify. The two regarded each other in bewilderment for a moment, the silence broken at last by the constable.

"It's all right my dear, I'm with Vinny."

"Vinny who?" enquired the face behind the bead curtains. It occurred to Jimmy that there was no point in any further explanation and a glance toward the car park gave confirmation to his suspicions. He thanked the woman for her trouble, leaving her with the reason for his visit to puzzle her for the remainder of her days.

The long walk to the road and through the outskirts of Todmorden to the road which would lead him to Manchester gave ample time for thought, and though he was concerned that he might be discovered by the local constabulary at any moment, his admiration for the cunning manner in which Vincent had revenged himself increased with every step taken. He waved down a car on the main road and its driver, having disclosed that he was on his way to within half a mile of where Jim should have been at that time, he accepted the offer of a lift. The driver, having allowed his insurance and tax to expire some weeks earlier, was more than pleased to get rid of his passenger before actually reaching the police station and Jimmy walked into the building only half an hour late.

Because he was a bandsman, there was none of the fuss that would have been made should one of us not turned up on time. Vincent and he were equal and the next time they met shook hands vigorously, after which, each made great play of counting their fingers.

Anyone not fortunate to be exempt from night work, and they were in the minority, had no idea what it was like to remain alert in the early hours of the morning; after all, the human body is at its lowest ebb around four and it is well known in medical circles that death is more likely to occur at that hour than at any other time. My own experience of that hour of low power has included actually falling asleep whilst walking my beat and finding myself on all fours in the street, my helmet rolling along in the gutter.

Some officers would stand in a shop doorway, prop their truncheon into the small of their back, against the door and doze off. The idea being, and it worked perfectly, that when they went to sleep, the truncheon would become dislodged and its clatter, as it fell to the floor, would wake them. I knew several others who carried small alarm clocks and got down to it in railway carriages, parked up in the sidings, thereby resting assured that they would not oversleep.

A constable who was on the same section as myself, was nicknamed 'Doormouse' and his speciality was to take a nap in a parked car. What few car owners there were in those days often neglected to lock the doors of their cars, so that there would always be a couple to choose from on most of the beats. One particularly wet morning at about four thirty he sought shelter in a car which was on the forecourt of a garage. He climbed into the rear seat, removed his dripping helmet and pulled his cape over his head for a little warmth and dozed off.

The officer awoke to feel the vehicle in motion and as he pulled his cape back, was horrified to see that the vehicle was being driven from the forecourt. He adjusted his helmet, at the same time tapping the driver on his shoulder he called for him to stop. The driver, understandably panicked and collided with a lamp post, thereby coming to a halt. At first the constable thought the driver was suffering from cardiac arrest as he was fighting for breath and clutching at his chest.

Eventually he calmed the poor fellow down and explained there had been a number of thefts from cars and finding his to be open, he concealed himself, hoping to catch any would be thief in the act. The damage to the car was slight and its owner thanked the officer for his diligence then carried on to work.

Chapter Nine

The bridge which carried the road from Cheetham into the city centre was the haunt of local prostitutes and their pimps. It was also a part of my beat in the spring of 1963, and at around ten in the evening I turned the corner to find it deserted, save for a well known pimp, who was sitting on the parapet of the bridge. The woman who relied on his protection, and a good hiding should she fail to earn a reasonable amount each evening, was probably entertaining a client nearby.

"Why are you hanging about here?" I asked.

"I can sit here if I want, it's nowt to do with you," he snarled.

I made a grab for him, intending to lock him up for obstructing the footpath and in an effort to avoid me he fell backwards from the parapet, disappearing from my view. As I looked down into the darkness below I heard a loud splash, he having entered the river from a thirty foot drop. I made my way down through several overgrown bombsites, picking my way, with some difficulty to the bank of the river.

The beam from my torch swept the fast flowing surface in an effort to discover the pimp, with negative result, and after a quarter of an hour I gave up and carried on with the beat. I went off duty at eleven, there being no word of the incident. The following afternoon, I paraded for duty and was told to attend the chief superintendent's office immediately.

I knocked on the office door and received the command to enter.I stood before the chief superintendent for some five minutes before he spoke.

"What have you been up to ?" he asked, without looking up from his desk.

"Well sir," I began, my mind racing with the idea that my adversary of the previous evening had been found drowned and that someone had witnessed the whole occurrence. "I have been working thirty seven beat for the past month."

He cut me short and fixing me with his famous stare, shouted that he wished to know the truth and that it would be most wise of me to tell him what I had been doing. I was of course, a seasoned officer with thirteen years service, spent dealing with every form of low life, both in and out of the job, a way of learning the trade that no amount of training schools could hope to achieve, and I was not about to succumb to this method of questioning.

I remained silent as he raved on, then he suddenly changed tack.

"If you won't tell me what you have been doing, you can tell the chief. Be at his office tomorrow morning at nine." he yelled, motioning me to leave him.

Outside the office, I met the chief inspector, who shook my hand and congratulated me.

"What for ?" I asked.

"Didn't he tell you, you're being promoted tomorrow," he informed me. I left the building in a daze. It had been almost eight years since I had passed the promotion qualification examination, and any thought of ever being made sergeant had long since been abandoned on my part. What form of pleasure was obtained by quizzing me in that way, I fail to identify.

Every police officer has a skeleton in the cupboard and perhaps it was hoped that I would reveal a couple of my own,
thereby blocking the promotion, I'll never know.
There I was, the next day, new stripes gleaming, outside the
office of the boss of the C Division at Mill Street Station.

"Come on in sergeant," called Chief Superintendent Fraser.
I hesitated for a moment, wondering where the sergeant was,
and realised it was me. Inside the office, Mr. Fraser, whom I
had known since his own days as a sergeant, shook my hand
and congratulated me on my promotion.

"I'm very glad to have you here," he said. "There's only two
kinds of officers here," he added. "Subnormal and severely
subnormal!"

I decided to wait and see for myself, and during the course
of the ensuing few months I discovered that he had been
right in only about twenty or thirty cases. On the strength of
the promotion, I moved, with my wife and first born, to a better class district and a spacious semi on a lovely secluded avenue in the New Moston area. I spent my annual leave moving
in and attempting to clear a somewhat neglected front garden,
where I looked up one afternoon to discover a young policeman standing at my gate.

"A thankless task isn't it," he grunted. I agreed and bent to
drive my spade deep into the clay.

"I'm just off to work; Oldham you know. That's Oldham bobbies, not Manchester. They haven't much idea them Manchester
lot, that's why I joined Oldham," he explained.

The officer went on to regale me with an account of his dis-
mounting from a bus at the corner of the avenue on the previous evening and having to deal with an accident on the
junction.

"On my way home off afternoons I was. Woman knocked over,
I stopped all the traffic." I glanced up from my digging to
find him displaying the number one stop signal, and a couple
of others which I didn't recognise. "Got someone to call an
ambulance and to inform Manchester, as it was in their area,"
the constable related. For the next ten minutes I received a full
report of the occurrence, culminating in the profuse apologies
of the Manchester Inspector who later had attended the scene.

"The inspector said I had done an excellent job and was
sorry I had been lumbered with it all, but all his officers had
been out of contact at the crucial time," he said, as he left me
to continue on his way to his duties.

A few days after our encounter, still on leave and strolling back from the local around two thirty in the afternoon I met the officer again. This time, he had just got off the bus and was walking behind me.

"Hello again," he bellowed, at which I halted to allow him to catch up with me. I enquired if he had finished for the day and was told that he had been to court and was back on duty that evening. As we walked along the main road towards our avenue, he described the arrest which had led to the court appearance.

"We get a lot of rough buggers up there," he said, pointing in the general direction of his force area. "This one gave me some abuse and I arrested him," said my companion. He took my arm and commenced to demonstrate the method he had employed in which to take his protesting prisoner to the station. He was of course in full uniform whilst I was in my gardening attire, and as the many motorists passed us, they could have all been forgiven for thinking that I was some miscreant he was dragging off to be locked up.

I managed to free myself from his iron grip before reaching my home, and after making some excuse I dashed into the house. About a week later, I was on my way to the bus stop in full uniform, when I spotted the Oldham bobby walking towards me.

"I didn't know you were in the job sergeant," he stammered."

"Well, after talking to you I decided to join," I said, and walked on. I never came into contact with the lad again. I think he used a roundabout way to get to the bus stop in an effort to avoid me.

In the weeks that followed, I moved on to the Levenshulme section, known throughout the rest of the division, as Sleepy Valley. Indeed there seemed little to do in comparison to the hurly burly of the other sections and one morning I decided to visit the home of an officer who was a sergeant on my former division. His wife admitted me and whispered that her husband was on nights and that he was in bed, fast asleep. She ushered me into the lounge and went off to make a cup of tea. I glanced around the sparsely furnished room and as she re entered the room, bearing a tray upon which was a teapot and cups, my gaze settled on a highly polished euphonium which was standing in a corner of the room.

"I had no idea that Bert was a musician," I said, nodding towards the instrument.

"He isn't," she said, pouring the tea and handing a cup to me.

"What happened was, a couple moved into next door about three years ago and kept playing loud music when he was in bed during the day, same as now. They said it wasn't their fault he worked nights and refused to turn it down." She walked over to the gleaming euphonium and polished its rim with her pinafore. "He bought this from one of those antique shops on Stockport Road and whenever he was on the evening shift, you know, coming home at two in the morning, he pressed it against next door's bedroom wall and blew very hard for about ten minutes."

I took a proffered biscuit and leaned back in the chair.

"Did it stop them playing the loud music?" I asked.

"Oh yes," she replied. "But he still gives 'em a tune if he's been to the pub." I asked her to let her husband know that I had been and took my leave. When I opened the gate I glanced at the adjacent house and noticed a 'For Sale ' sign in the front garden.

As I finished my tour in Sleepy Valley and moved over to the Gorton Section, the winds of change were but a gentle breeze that by the end of the year were to develop into a gale. It heralded the slow death of the police force and by the end of 1967 it was gone for ever.

The main contributor to its demise was a scheme put forward by the faceless ones who wander the corridors of Whitehall. Every Chief Constable of England and Wales was asked by the Home Office whether they would like to have all their officers working their beats in cars, the vehicles to be supplied by that office, at no expense to their respective Police Authority.

The offer was accepted by one and all and the vehicles were delivered. Manchester's fleet were the Morris 1000 model, painted in blue and white with the sign 'Police' on the roof. Once accepted by the force, there followed the announcement from the government that as each car was to cover six beats, six officers were to be got rid of, and that to be achieved by natural wastage. Within a very short time, the bobby walking the street disappeared and with him, all personal contact with the public.

Hitherto, as we strolled through thickly populated areas, we would be constantly approached by people who wished to tell us what was happening, like a full report on a member of the family in hospital, the forthcoming celebration of another's birthday, together with an invitation to attend. I have even been asked to be Godfather to a child who was born in my presence, having been called in from the beat by a panicking father. There was a wealth of information to be had from these sources with regard to the nefarious activities of some of the neighbours. The occupants of those tightly packed streets went to bed at night, content that the policeman would always be within callingdistance should the need arise.

Once an officer got into one of the new fangled Panda Cars, as they became known, there was no way of getting him out of it until the end of the shift, particularly during inclement weather. As a sergeant, although there was a car available, I resisted the facility always preferring to be on foot. My decision was helped when a new set of rules was produced involving the invention of the breathalyser.

A few weeks before it was brought into use, the inspectors attended a short course in its application with the idea of instructing we sergeants, who in turn would train the constables. I came into the station at two in the morning in order to take my refreshments having earlier accepted the invitation of a local publican to join him in a night cap or two.

The inspector was toying with a green plastic box, from which he withdrew a glass tube. "I want to show you how this thing works," he said as he snapped off the ends of the tube. He fitted a mouthpiece over one end and on the other, he placed a plastic bag.

"You ask the motorist to take a deep breath and then blow up the bag, as he would a balloon. Do you see in the tube, there are yellow crystals. Now if he has been drinking alcohol those crystals will turn to green, then you arrest him," he explained.

I thanked him and turned to go into the dining room, at which he held out the bag to me and gestured for me to blow up the bag as part of the demonstration. After several protestations I was unable to escape his insistence and blew long and hard into the bag.

"It's turned green right up to the end," he said. The Charge Office Clerk, a friend of mine, announced that the other divisions had found a number of the instruments to be faulty and that got me off the hook. I mentioned that my coffee was getting cold and withdrew to the dining room. After supper I left by the back door and kept out of the way until signing off at seven. When I came into the station, the Inspector informed me that the whole batch of breathalysers were faulty and that he had packed them off back to headquarters with a nasty note.

"Yes, I got every officer who came in to blow in the bag and in every case the crystals changed to green!" he said

"It's a good job we didn't try them out on the public," I said. That small incident was influential in my decision to stay on foot and if I wanted a ride round, to get one of my men to pick me up.

Superimposed on the normal beats, were constables who were Community Officers and their role was that of close contact with the public. They covered quite large areas and were more or less freelance, in that they chose their own hours of working and often did so in plain clothes. George, an officer with some six years service, was one of those men. He was very keen and I gave him my backing in anything he did. He telephoned me when I came into the station one Friday night, and informed me that he was at a fish and chips restaurant where the proprietor had experienced disorderly behaviour from drunken youths throughout the evening.

"I'm in plain clothes serge and inside the place know. The restaurant is full of the bastards and there's trouble coming."

I told him to hang on and not to let them know who he was and a moment or two later I had all six men on my section, in the van and heading for George with myself following, driven in a Panda Car by another officer. As the van turned into the street on which the restaurant was situated, I saw that a large group of youths were fighting both inside and outside the premises.

We piled in immediately and within a short time began to fill the van. I set about punching a few heads and my lads followed my example. One of the hooligans was particularly active as he belted anyone who was within his reach and as he was obviously the ring leader, I made for him. I pulled his anorak over his head and dragged him across the street where I thumped him and threw him into the van.

I looked around to discover the fighting was over and the remainder of the mob had run off so I ordered the packed van to Whitworth Street Station. When I arrived the van was being emptied and the miscreants were being taken in to the Charge Office. I looked into the dark interior of the vehicle and saw that one of the prisoners was underneath the seats. I went in to drag him out when he said, "It's me serge,

George."

The bundle extricated itself from beneath its cramped haven and stood up. I asked him how he got there and he informed me that it was I who had belted him and tossed him in.

"My bloody radio was blaring away under my coat and I had to get under there before they worked out it was me who was behind it all," he said.

It was just an example of down to earth police work, as I explained to him afterwards, but my later attempt to further his career also ended up a bit of a disaster.

The Chief Constable, having received several complaints from one of the hundreds of night-club proprietors operating in the city in the nineteen sixties, as to the unlawful activities of his competitors, decided to bring matters to the fore and if the complaints proved to be well founded, act accordingly.

The allegations were to the effect that although some of the clubs had been granted exemption from the strict permitted hours regulations, they were not complying to law. Those regulations allowed the Licensing Justices to grant an extension of hours in which alcoholic drinks may be supplied, to those clubs which had satisfied them as to the law.

The law, at that time, was to the effect that, provided there were table meals to be had and a proper kitchen where they may be prepared, the customers may be supplied with intoxicating liquor, as being ancillary to that meal, until two o'clock in the morning. These regulations, as pointed out by the disgruntled complainant, were being well and truly flouted and drinking went on in those establishments, without meals and until dawn.

The plan was to gather evidence of these offences and to present them at the court as each club proprietor came to court, annually to renew his licence, thereby opposing the renewals and effectively closing them down, one by one.

A scheme evolved wherein a unit of police officers were to go undercover and infiltrate the drinking dens in order to gather the required evidence. Those officers selected for the covert operations, were required to be of physical appearance which would be unlikely to arouse suspicion as to who they were, and they became known to the rest of the force, as the Hush Puppies. They were subject to strict rules, being required to arrive at the city centre station for nine in the evening and to turn up there at four in the morning when they wrote and submitted their reports before retiring.

As they would be obliged to take alcohol during their observations, they were not permitted to come and go in their own vehicles and a taxi was laid on for transport to and from work. Each evening, the individual officers were briefed as to which club they were to conduct observations, and to, at all costs, to avoid revealing the fact that they were the police.

Within a few weeks there accumulated sufficient evidence to oppose the renewal of licences and by the end of some eighteen months, the night-club business in Manchester was dead and buried, never to come back.

In later years, a form of night-club scene emerged, but the various venues had no need to rely on the sale of drink, more the ability of its customers to writhe around a dance floor, having brought their own stimulants with them. George, who had been the victim of friendly fire at the fish and chip restaurant, had been chosen for a Hush Puppy and as enthusiastically as ever, he was determined to make the best of it.

"Your club is Brockingams tonight," whispered the inspector. "You know what to do, off you go."

George, who was unfamiliar with the division, had some difficulty in tracing the establishment and it was after ten when he descended the gloomy staircase which led from the back street to the door of the club. Two or three knocks brought what seemed to be a gorilla in an evening suit.

"You a member?" asked the gorilla.

George announced that he was in town on business and that the club had been recommended to him, at which he was allowed to pass inside. He was, to some extent, glad of the poor lighting inside and on arrival at the bar, realised he was the first customer of the evening. He ordered a glass of beer and sat down at the bar where he took a sip from the glass commensurable with a shortage of cash and about five hours hanging around in the place.

Gradually, more and more customers filled the empty tables and having toyed with an empty glass for as long as he could without drawing attention to himself, he indicated to the barman that he was ready for a refill.

"I'll get that," said someone at his side. He turned to find a young attractive girl in a silvery trouser suit smiling at him. He could have very well done without the girl's effort to engage him in conversation but went along with it so as not to draw any undue attention to himself, and so he decided to at least, be pleasant.

The sweet young thing was pouting and displaying a body language which, as a happily married man, left him uneasy to say the least and it was only his devotion to duty which delayed him from quitting the scene immediately.

By eleven o'clock he had complied with his companion's request to dance with her on three occasions and was on his third glass of beer when she confessed that she was, in fact, a male. It dawned on him that he had detected some effeminacy amongst everyone around the bar, but he had been completely taken aback by the person who was now gripping his arm.

"Don't look round but my boyfriend has just come in. He's always jealous of me and thinks it's big to take it out of anyone else Imight like," said the sweet young thing.

George turned and was faced with an ugly brute of gigantic proportions, who by the way he was snarling and striking the clenched fist of his right hand into the palm of the other, seemed to bear out the observations of his boy friend.

"Well, I've got a train to catch," said George as he moved off towards the exit. The Town Hall Clock was striking half past eleven as he strolled into Deansgate and having spent his allocated expenses, faced four hours to kill before presenting himself at headquarters. Wearily, he at long last sat down in the office to write his report, after which he climbed in to his taxi and went home.

The next evening, on arrival at the office, the superintendent called him over.

"Your club last night was that new gay one wasn't it?" he said. "I note from your report that all was in order when you left at two fifteen, the bar having closed at two, no incidents or anything untoward," said the superintendent, reading from George's observations of the previous night.

"That is correct sir," said the officer.

"Then you didn't notice Sergeant Armstrong and his plain clothes team raiding the premises at midnight?" enquired the superintendent.

George had no explanation and was forced to confess to leaving the place early. Because the activities of the 'hush puppies' were to be kept under wraps, George was not the subject of any disciplinary proceedings and was merely returned to his division and to my section.

He was not disappointed. "The wife was getting a bit fed up with me living it up in clubs all night, as she liked to put it," he told me.

"Well at least you weren't dancing the night away with any women," I said.

The rest of the constables on my section at that time were, as everywhere, a mixed bunch, a weird arrangement I had come across during my first couple of days in the army.

On my arrival at Ballykinlar Barracks in Northern Ireland, those many years previously, we were split up into squads of thirty and allotted a barrack room. In each of those rooms there was a bully, a scruffy individual, a smart lad, a bloke who took to drill and general military life as if born for it, a comedian, an excessive grumbler, a religious type and an atheist, somebody who was lovesick and another home sick. There were bright ones and thick ones, athletes and someone too bone idle for any physical activity, all of whom were seventeen or eighteen years of age.

My point is that there were ten such barrack rooms housing the group that arrived on the same day as myself. Why was there not one room full of comedians, another housing only bullies, another in which only smart men could be found and so on? Had computers been invented I might have believed the arrangements, per barrack room had been made scientifically but they hadn't and I was left with the phenomenon, which was ever present throughout my army career, and now albeit to a lesser extent in my police days.

In the main I had a good set of policemen under my command, though one was a disappointment to say the least. His nickname was 'Captain Fearless', from a boy's periodical of the day, and I discovered why when I encountered him on nights for the first time.

I was somewhere in the middle of his beat around two in the morning, when I heard a merry tune being loudly whistled and saw the beam of a torch which was dancing about the road and occasionally, into the doorways of shops. The whistler drew near and I saw it was 'Captain Fearless', who greeted me with, "All correct, sergeant!"

I told him I wasn't surprised and that his advertising his presence so openly must have warned every burglar for miles. That of course was his object as he was terrified he might have to arrest one. He pointed out that he was preventing crime with his manner of working and of course he was right; nevertheless, I insisted he must go about it with a bit more stealth.

Some of the 'Captain's' colleagues had experienced difficulty when tackling angry men and discovering that he had disappeared during the ensuing melee. There was a general desire to bring him to heel and a plan was hatched when he was moved on to a beat upon which it was necessary to pass through a large cemetery.

One of the constables, later in life to become a well known actor, particularly for his role in 'Coronation Street', borrowed a shroud from the station mortuary. He hid behind a gravestone and with the garment over his head, lay in wait for the timid officer's footsteps on the gravel path. He heard, and saw the quarry approach and at the most effective moment, stood up, waved his arms and groaned. He had applied his expertise as a thespian, certainly as far as his victim was concerned, who, with a blood curdling scream, retraced his footsteps at an incredible speed towards the safety of the brightly illuminated main road and still travelling at top speed, to the station.

When the 'ghost' had resumed his beat, he heard that 'Captain Fearless' had reported sick. He was off duty for a fortnight and returned to take up duty on a different section, so that I had no further contact with him. I daresay that in these present times he would have received counselling and been given a job which avoided night duty, but there you are.

Chapter Ten

I stood at the busy junction of Ardwick Green on a foggy morning in November and tried to appear to be interested in the frustration of motorists as they struggled to negotiate the roundabout. The odd sounds being produced by my stomach were calling me to the station for breakfast, which, in the shape of a couple of eggs presented to me by one of the local butchers, was hidden beneath my helmet.

As I turned to leave I was approached by two very untidy individuals, one of whom said that they were escapees from Sudbury Open Prison and that they wished to surrender to me. To my annoyance, in view of what would now be a delay in dining, I told them to follow me to the station which was half a mile away. I sat both men down in the dining room and instructed the officer who was in charge of the general duties, cells, mortuary, and so on, to boil my eggs and make a jug of tea.

Whilst I waited for those culinary duties to be carried out, I asked the fugitives to relate the facts of matter. Duncan, the spokesman, and Ken, his companion, had been serving a sentence of two years for theft and were cellmates in the institution.

"It was my idea really," said Duncan. "We had been on a working party all week, you know, clearing a canal of rubbish, and as there wasn't much of what you might call, supervision, so I asked Ken here if he would do a bunk with me."

"I said OK, and a week last Friday we just strolled away and walked a couple of miles to the village," added Ken.

The eggs having been placed before me I got on with my refreshments and told the Charge Office Clerk to contact the prison and get them to send someone up for them.

"Where have you been since then?" I enquired. They informed me that when their plan was revealed to others they were in receipt of boundless advice, most of it being useless, though the suggestion of one prisoner, Jacko, that they should make for Manchester and his home address sounded like a good idea.

"Tell the wife Jacko sent yer and that she's got to put you up for a few days," said the benefactor. The plan worked well and their absence went undiscovered for some five hours by which time they had taken a car from a cinema car park and were heading north.

"Ken was moaning about being hungry so when I saw a little post office come grocery store I bobbed in. There was nobody about so I pushed a few chocolate bars into my pocket and when I turned to leave, I spotted a big green bag on the counter so I lifted that as well," said Duncan.

In answer to my query, as to the contents of the bag, both said, "about three grand."

I asked where the money was now and they told me it had all been spent, and that was partly the reason they had given themselves up. Having found Jacko's address on the fourth floor of a block of flats in one of those run down council estates, they dumped their transport and knocked on the door. The physical appearance of the lady of the house belied that description given by her ever loving spouse, apparently a symptom of those suffering from a long period of incarceration.

She bore the features of having descended from generations of low breeding and possessed that demeanour which seems to be obligatory to such individuals.

74

"He told us she was beautiful," said Duncan, in a tone of disgust.

"Rough as a bear's arse more like!" endorsed Ken.

The lads went on to tell me that she was refusing them sanctuary until they revealed their good fortune and permitted her a glance at the cash.

"After that she went all coy and let us inside," said Ken. They spent the next few days and all their money, confined to the gross untidiness of the council flat

"She said that her sister lived a couple of floors below and asked if she could join us, as her partner was away as well," said Duncan. "Between the pair of 'em they cleaned us out, although they were very obliging in the you know what department."

Some of the money went on beer, wine and gin, but most of it went on designer clothes and the hairdressers, they told me.

"Anyway, this morning, when we said the money was all gone, she told us to go or she was ringing the police, so we cleared out. We walked about for a time and then saw you sarge," said Ken.

The officers from the prison eventually collected them both and that was the end of the matter as far as I was concerned. I had, of course, informed the force which covered the location of the stolen mail bag and that was that. A day or so later I called at the address given as their temporary hiding place and put the fear of God up their former hostess. She of course denied any knowledge of the men and their money, but the flat was exactly as described, including the stomach churning stink therein.

"Well I'm going to inform your husband and your sister's boyfriend when they get out," was my parting shot. Naturally I never did.

Within the few weeks that followed, I commenced what was to turn out the remainder of my career as Detective Sergeant at the C.I.D. office of the C. Division. Here there was plenty of work for the understaffed department, the division being similarly populated as the one I had left behind a couple of years before. There was much crime to be detected and had we understood the term stress, or pressure, we would have realised why it was that the pub across the street was so popular.

My being new to the office exposed me to the usual practical jokes, as when I discovered a white coat with a stethoscope hanging from a pocket, in a cupboard.

"Oh that's in case anyone we're interviewing happens to ask to see a doctor," explained one of the Detective Constables. A similar explanation that a barrister's wig and gown I discovered in a drawer was to appease someone asking to see a lawyer made no impression on me, at least I never saw those commodities employed.

The pub across the road, was known as the detective's trough and at any time, day or night, several of the sleuths could be found at the bar. The Detective Superintendent himself was more than a regular and would demand the presence of his staff on a regular basis. I was there on one such occasion when he introduced me to an acquaintance of his.

"He's got a bit of a problem with his lad. Have a chat with him," was his command.

"He's sixteen and I think he's got in with a bad lot," said the doting parent. He reeled off a catalogue of minor occurrences, like stealing from his mother's purse, coming in at all hours of the morning and hurling abuse when taken to task. I asked what it was he would like me to do and he suggested I had him down to the station to frighten him.

It was around that time that the do-gooders were gaining strength with their liberal attitudes and sneaking themselves into key jobs in Whitehall, a strategy which in later years was to prove a disaster for law and order throughout the land, and the old methods which had proved so effective during my earlier service were giving way to rampant lawlessness.

In view of that state of affairs, when by arrangement, his father brought the lad to see me on a Saturday afternoon, I decided to have a quiet chat with him, sending his dad home with a promise that I would deliver him to his home some time later. The station was of early Victorian design with a strangely depressing interior, with one long corridor of cells which were in constant use and another in which the cells were rarely occupied.

It was along the latter that I propelled the errant youth and locking him in the furthest cell I began to lecture him upon the error of his recent ways. He was arrogant and I was about to chastise him further when I was called away to the telephone. There had been a shooting incident and I was required to attend at once. On arrival at the scene I was informed that the victim was dead, having been gunned down on his doorstep.

I became heavily engaged in the affair and it was around two in the morning when I fell exhausted into my bed. I rose at ten, it was Sunday and the murder enquiry was being conducted by others, so I settled down to a quiet day off. Half way through breakfast, I was called to the telephone. The caller was the Charge Office Sergeant.

"I've tried everyone else Dennis," he said apologetically. "Did you happen to notice one of the detectives put a lad in the cells yesterday?" he asked. "I happened to be in the old cell corridor when I heard him crying and he told me a detective had locked him in yesterday."

I confessed immediately and asked him to get him out, to give him a cup of tea and said I would be there forthwith. The youth was a shadow of his former arrogance and during the journey to his home I explained that if he thought one night in a cell was unpleasant, a couple of years would be purgatory, and that would be his fate if he failed to behave in the future. The reunion with his mother was highly emotional and after ascertaining that there would be no come back as far as I was concerned, I went home to enjoy the remainder of my Sunday off.

Some months after the 'cure' the boss mentioned that his friend had thanked him for altering his son, who apparently, literally, overnight, had been transformed into a model and dutiful boy by myself.

"How did you manage that?" he asked.

"You don't want to know," I replied. He was a shrewd man and he walked away whistling.

Some of the newly introduced rules of cautioning individuals involved not only the persistent offenders with the protection of youth on their side, but the elderly, in certain circumstances.

One of the detective constables based at my station happened to be in the proximity of a corner shop when the proprietor was seen to be standing outside the premises holding a little old lady by her wrist.

"I caught her stealing a tin of soup from the shop," said Mr. Shazeen, the shopkeeper. The officer handed back the stolen can and told the complainant that if he should be in agreement, he would see to it that the old girl got a caution and that he would ensure that she kept out of his establishment in the future. Mr. Shazeen said that he would be satisfied with that method of dealing with the matter and the D.C. walked on a few yards with the shoplifter.

At the corner, he told her never to enter the shop again and left her for more pressing matters on the patch. Two weeks later the superintendent called him in to his office.

"Feller called Shazeen has been on to me, wants to know how I went on with cautioning some old girl you dealt with, I cant find any reports on it." snarled the superintendent.

The detective said that there had been a delay due to the miscreant having been ill and that the report and application for the official cautioning was to be submitted by him that very day.

"I'll see her on Friday," decided the boss, dismissing the officer with a wave of his hand. He had three days to find the old woman, whose name and address he hadn't bothered to obtain and an afternoon spent trying to trace her drew a blank. Two or three bitters served to concentrate his troubled mind and a desperate plan took shape. Later that evening, he travelled to Chester and the home of his mother, and here, after an account of what had happened, he outlined the manner in which his mother could save him from that terrible punishment of being returned to uniformed duties.

"And so you see mam, if you could pretend to be that old woman and just stand in front of my boss whilst he cautions you, I'll still be in the C.ID.," he pleaded.

His mother's reaction was to be outraged. Not so much that she was being asked to carry out such an outrageous deception, but at the suggestion that she, at only sixty three years of age, could get away with the role of an old woman.

Further pleading and the fact that she had for some years been involved in amateur dramatics at the church hall, found her changing her mind.

"I could wear that suit I got for your wedding and a new pair of shoes I saw in town last week and ..."

"Whoa mother!" said her son. "The woman you're supposed to be is in poor circumstances and probably hasn't had a new suit or a fresh pair of shoes for years."

Another couple of hours found her accepting the challenge with faint traces of enthusiasm, partly as it would be rescuing her son from a fate worse than death and partly because she believed she had always been meant to follow a successful career on the stage.

On the following Friday, she was marched into the superintendent, who went through the ritual of telling her that he had decided not to put her before the court, but instead to caution her with regard to her stealing a can of soup. He looked at the sorry sight before him, who had gone somewhat over the top in her choice of wardrobe for the part, not least the unkempt and obvious wig and worn out slippers. She looked vaguely familiar to him and he tried to recall where he may have seen her before.

"Were you one of Glasgow Mary's girls at one time?" he asked. She shook her head to indicate that she wasn't and her son, fervently hoping that he didn't elaborate, asked if that was all.

"Yes, take her to the canteen and give the poor old bugger a cup of tea," said the boss.

The D.C., only too relieved to have weathered the interview, rushed his mother down the stairs and into his car. On the journey to Chester he was asked for an opinion on her acting ability and he congratulated her.

"I cant wait to tell everyone at church," said his mother.

"No, don't do that; promise me you wont tell anyone," said her boy.

"Alright, maybe just one or two," she muttered. It was almost a year before the detective felt sure the matter would remain a secret and he never again let anyone off, old lady or not.

Chapter Eleven

Alcohol has been the downfall of a great many uniformed police officers. The C.I.D., however, thrived on it as almost a necessity. As most criminals seemed to spend their ill gotten gains in drinking establishments it was essential that sleuths also resorted to them, in the constant pursuit of information. Many detectives cultured informants, or snouts, as they were referred to, and indeed there existed a small sum of money from which payments were made to these snouts, usually when some major crime was being investigated.

In less serious matters, the information would be forthcoming through the detective's own pocket, in the form of a glass of beer to be proffered to the snout. A number of the grasses, as the underworld called them, did it for the pure joy of the thing and either way, it produced results. A detective is only as good as his information, is an old saying and is very true.

One of my own snouts, I shall call Malcolm, was a professional thief and if he had directed his inventiveness towards some honourable calling, I feel he would have prospered in the world. As it was, he died penniless at the age of fifty nine, twenty five of those years spent at the Sovereign's pleasure.

After, I had retired from the police force, I was employed by a large department store group, and whilst on the shop floor, I spotted Malcolm amongst the shoppers. There seemed something odd about his manner, though he was, as always, immaculate in appearance. He had, on an occasion, explained to me that he often wandered about in office buildings, with the purpose of finding an office temporarily abandoned by some female member of staff, she having left her hand bag in the room.

"I made a few quid at that game," he told me. "Of course I was always ham boned up, nice suit on, clean shirt and all that. If anyone turned up while I was where I shouldn't be, I apologised, said I was looking for a mister so and so and they accepted it."

Now here was Malcolm, carrying a large gift wrapped parcel before him and holding it with both out stretched arms. He hadn't seen me as I popped behind a display of coats and he arrived at a counter which dealt in expensive cameras. He placed the box on the edge of the counter whilst he engaged in merely looking at the various products. At the approach of the assistant he thanked her and said that he was just looking. As Malcolm turned away I was right behind him.

"Hello Mister Wood," he greeted me. "Doing a bit of shopping?" he asked.

"No, but I see you are. Let's have a look at your box," I said, as I walked him to the security room. The arms which supported his load turned out to be those of a tailor's dummy, and the box, containing stolen merchandise, included watches from our store. He had devised the stealing tool himself, it having a hinged base and with his real hands free, underneath his immaculate raincoat, he was able to select the items and pack them away without any suspicion on behalf of the assistants.

Malcolm wasn't pleased to hear that I was no longer a copper, but there you are. So it seemed, that all in all, the boozing aspect was indeed justifiable on the part of the detective branch, after all, who could say that the two large men, wearing trilby hats and trench macs, propping up the bar in some inn of ill repute were police officers? On the other hand, there would be little room for doubt if they were in full uniform including helmets

As I said, the uniformed officers were at a disadvantage when they desired to quench their raging thirst and were constantly in danger of being caught by one or other of their supervisory ranks. Most hostelries, however, were fairly safe, particularly at night and when the customers had drifted off to their homes. There were always those who would go over the top and be disciplined for it. There was a rule, that if the whole force got through the Christmas and New Year holiday without any police officer being done for drinking on duty, then everyone would be awarded an extra day's leave to be taken in the ensuing months. Of course there was always someone who would break the rule, and it was often said that the Watch Committee had promised the day off in the certain knowledge that the members of the force would never qualify for it.

One festive season however came dangerously close, when New Year's Eve arrived and there had been no offender.

Police constable A 111, Arthur Russell had been serving for fifteen years, a career unblemished, largely in view of his strict temperance, a condition attributed to the foresight of his mother during his early childhood, who had enrolled her small boy into the Racabite Society, a group whose purpose it was, to commit the young to a lifetime of abstinence.

The youngster, then in middle age, was indeed a firm teetotaller and the section sergeant, who visited him in Oldham Street at one-o'clock in the afternoon of New Year's Eve, found the officer, as was to be expected, completely free of any signs of drink. At two o'clock, Russell failed to appear at Albert Street Police Station with the rest of his shift, to retire from duty, and at three, a search was organised in case he was lying injured somewhere on his beat.

At half past four, he walked in to the station wearing civilian clothes, and very drunk. The inspector sent for the superintendent, who interviewed the inebriated constable, a task which proved extremely difficult as the interviewee insisted on serenading his superior officer with a large repertoire of risqué songs from his previous career in the Cheshire Regiment.

The more he was ordered to be quiet, the louder the singing, until the superintendent wearied of it and ordered two plainclothes men to take him home and suspended him. Those officers were away for some time and on their return, described to the superintendent the great difficulty they had experienced in taking the inebriated constable home.

"He kept up that singing sir," said the first plain clothes man.

"And he insisted on leaving the tram at every junction, in order to direct the traffic."

His colleague added, "the tram driver said he would call the next policeman he saw if the three of us didn't get off his tram, and after I whispered that we were the police, he informed the rest of the passengers in a loud voice to that effect."

The superintendent enquired as to what action the men had taken, and they disclosed that they left the vehicle and supporting the drunken officer under the armpits, continued on foot for the last mile or so, the last few yards to the fellow's address attracting much curiosity from the immediate neighbours and the embarrassment of the constable's wife.

Three days into the new year, the unfortunate officer was in attendance at the office of the Chief Constable, where, invited to give an explanation, he made a statement to the effect that on the fateful afternoon, he had passed the time of day with the driver of a mineral water delivery cart. The driver had given him a bottle of mineral water which he had consumed in an entry on his beat. The contents, it now appeared, were some form of strong drink, probably gin.

"The next thing I remembered, was waking up at home on new year's day," he said.

The constable was required to resign forthwith.

There was little sympathy from anyone, some thinking, "there but for the grace of God," maybe. But in the main, he was cursed as the agent of yet another season of cheer, for which there would be no extra day awarded.

Chapter Twelve

Offences of an indecent nature were dealt with by the Plain Clothes Department, a group, usually six in number, headed by a sergeant. The department was also concerned with betting and gaming, the licensing laws, Sunday trading and entertainment, prostitution and the statutory assaults, wounding and the like. I served in that department both as a constable and as a sergeant.

My introduction to the indecency side came within the first month of my stint as a constable, when I was directed to attend one of the new and trendy, Unisex Hairdressing Salons which were springing up in the late nineteen fifties. The manager of the shop had telephoned our department after one of her staff noticed a client behaving indecently whilst having a haircut. On my arrival the place was in an uproar, with all the salon's girls talking at once and the manager bathing a nasty gash on the top of the alleged offender's head.

"I've rung for an ambulance," stammered the agitated manager as I bent to examine the wound and pronounce it superficial. After quietening everyone down I sought an explanation and took the girl who had been dealing with the injured man to one side.

"The customer came in and I was free, so I asked him to sit in the chair. I placed the cover over him and fastened it at the back of his neck in the usual manner, then, after asking him what style he required, I began to brush his hair from behind him of course."

"Then what happened?" I enquired.

"Well, I saw his hands moving under the cover, they were going up and down in very fast jerky movements. We get plenty of weirdos in here and I thought to myself, how dare he do that to me."

I enquired as to what the man was doing and her reply was to the effect that he was using her in some perverted fantasy.

"I went mad and my reaction was to hit him hard on the top of his filthy head with my hairbrush and to pull the cover off him."

"And what did you see?" I asked, with some embarrassment
"The poor man was cleaning his glasses," interrupted the manager.
"Not polishing anything else then?" I asked.
It became clear that there had been a mistake made and the injured client accepted everything good humouredly.
"Just shows you girls, things are not always what they seem to be," I said.

For the man on the beat, constantly seeking to escape the boredom of walking round a comparatively quiet area at night, there was the occasional view of someone preparing to retire having neglected to switch off the bedroom light and to draw the curtains. It was often suspected that the practice was deliberate, knowing that the constable would be round about at the crucial moment, as was made evident by the striking of elaborate poses, quite unnecessary in the ordinary routine of undressing.

A number of other activities took place which any officer who was working his beat enthusiastically, could not fail to observe, as he patrolled the rear entries of the myriad terraced houses on his beat. Any unusual light or noise would cause the officer to look over a back yard gate in order to ensure that all was well, and from time to time, he would be confronted with a liaison taking place in a ground floor room, the participants in which, having seen fit to leave the light on and the curtains open, could be seen cavorting in full view.

One such performance took place, with such regularity, as to become a bore to the regular officers on the beat and was more or less ignored. One of my colleagues, who was on that particular beat for some twelve months had long since bothered looking over the yard gate, when he had occasion to board a bus, and placing himself on one of those rear seats which face each other, looked across at a young man and woman who were sitting directly opposite to him and greeted them profusely. When the pair half-heartedly returned the greeting, it struck him that try as he might, he was unable to recall their names, nor indeed, where he knew them from.

After a couple of stops he left the bus and a minute later remembered them. He had never seen them with their clothes on, nor even spoken to them.

"I often wonder if they are still together, and still wonder who the bloody hell I was," said my colleague when I met him years later.

There is, and always will be, another category of sexual offender, who is a source of amusement to most males, and sometimes, though not always, to females. He is 'The Flasher', and he gets his buzz from exposing his person to the ladies. I have prosecuted dozens of these miscreants and tried to discover the thinking behind their practises, in vain.

A book was kept at all plain clothes offices, into which was entered every complaint of flashing on the division. The name of the complainant was written, the time and place of the incident, and a description of the offender. That book was regularly examined by the Divisional Commander who would demand that outstanding reports, and that's not a pun, were followed up in an effort to discover the perpetrator and get him charged.

The problem with sexual offenders, is that, unlike someone who goes around breaking other men's noses, or burgling shops and houses, or committing any other type of skulduggery, he doesn't like anyone whatsoever to know what he does and in consequence, there is no one to grass on him. That makes it extremely difficult to obtain the necessary evidence in order to successfully prosecute him.

The problem is even greater when, as often is the case, the man is a paedophile whose victims are far too young to give evidence on oath and he of course is reluctant to confess to his heinous crimes. In the case of the flasher, the complainant will sometimes recognise him as being someone known to her, maybe at work, or a neighbour for instance. Such men tend to indulge in the stealing of items of underwear from washing lines and a visit to their homes would often reveal that behaviour on a large scale.

I knew one of these characters quite well and discovered, early in our acquaintanceship, his habit of wearing a long raincoat, in all weather conditions. Underneath that garment, he was naked, with the exception of trouser legs from ankle to knee, where they were secured by elastic bands. His *modus operandi* was to confront the ladies and open wide the raincoat, thereby providing the maximum of exposure.

One pleasant spring morning it was reported to me that a young woman had been exposed to in a novel manner whilst she had been carrying out her part time job, that of delivering washing powder samples through the letter boxes of terraced

85

houses on the division. She told me that it was her method to deliver at the odd numbered side of each street then to continue on the even numbered side.

"I came to the last house, which was number two," she told me. "And when I pushed the sample into the letterbox, I thought I had brushed against the arm of a tiny tot. When I withdrew my hand from the letterbox I was horrified to see a man's 'wotsit' appear through the same slot!"

I went to the house with the woman and asked her to place another sample in the same manner has she had previously done, and this she did. There was some shuffling on the inside and the door was opened to reveal a man of around thirty, completely bare and apparently most excited at the return of the young woman.

At the station, his explanation was to the effect that he had heard the tapping of the woman's high heeled shoes on the pavement and seeing what she was doing, calculated that she would eventually arrive at his address.

"I thought that if I stood behind the door with nothing on, she would touch me, which she did. I couldn't help pushing through the letterbox. When I heard her heels again and her rattling the letterbox, I thought she had returned because she enjoyed it."

He had certainly been disappointed when he saw me there as well as his victim and the magistrates, having learned that he was a merchant seaman, due to sail the next day, gave him a conditional discharge, but not before, as a favour to me, he asked for ten previous offences to be taken into consideration in my area.

The chief superintendent was overjoyed when he saw the number of flashing cases detected that month. Not that the gentlemen perverts had it their own way, by any means. We were called on many occasions to an area of derelict land to the rear of Strangeways Prison, where a young lady who was well known to the police, made a habit of stripping off all her clothing and cavorting up and down in view of the prisoners, hundreds of whom would be at the windows of their cells, whooping and cheering until the whole institution and immediate environs became alarmed, the zenith of the performance being the arrival of the beat man and his, often futile efforts, to detain the star of the show.

There would be a deal of running up and down the undulated stage and when very occasionally, the officer came to grips with his quarry, she would slip from his grasp, there being no garment to hold on to.

What with the deafening chorus of booing from the captive audience, at his attempts to detain the stripper, coupled with the frustrations of those denied the pleasure of female companionship for so long, the chase would be called off, allowing the offender to escape until the next time.

The prison staff made an unofficial request for the officer on the beat, taking in the prison, to find something else to do when repeat performances were made and in the main, we obliged.

Prostitution will always be with us, and no amount of legislation will ever stop it. Actually being a prostitute is not against the law and a woman who wishes to accept money from a man in return for sexual practises, is quite within her rights. It is when she solicits for that purpose, in a public place that she begins to offend.

Whilst looking in to the activities of a man suspected of living off the earnings of a prostitute, I had occasion to speak to the lady concerned. She had become disenchanted with the fellow, who had, at first befriended her, then had begun to knock her about when she failed to earn enough money for him. The man was suspected of having the control of several other prostitutes to whom he also delivered beatings when they had not worked hard enough for him.

I have never understood why these girls allow a man to take their often dangerously earned wages from them, and to put up with such bestial behaviour from that same individual. That particular girl was prepared to help in the prosecution of the pimp, and after some weeks of difficulty, my colleagues and I had him convicted and sent to prison. I advised him to go and live in some other town whenever he was released, and he, understanding me perfectly, did just that.

His erstwhile victim became a very good informer and we were able to prosecute a lot of brothel keepers who would otherwise have been ahead of the law.

My snout, on my advice, purchased a small house in the area and after I outlined to her that she was perfectly within the law to take men there for her lewd practises, for payment, she must never allow any of her pals to use the premises in the same way.

For a building to qualify as a brothel, it must be resorted to by two or more women. The girl followed my further advice and drew her clients from men who were in business and entertained them purely by appointment either at her address or at their office.

Until 1959, when a new law, The Street Offences Act, came into power, the prostitutes were arrested regularly and on a semi rotary basis, and charged with 'obstructing the footpath'. They attended court the next day and happily paid a fine, which they treated as a sort of mild taxation, in the knowledge that they were not due again for a week or so. I and other members of the plain clothes department attended the area of Piccadilly in the city centre, at twenty minutes to midnight on the eve of the Act coming into effect.

As normal, there was a prostitute every two or three yards, all around Piccadilly and along nearby York Street, some forty or fifty girls, each jealously guarding their own pitch, their ponces lurking nearby, a scene which had gone on for many years.

At two minutes to midnight, they all disappeared, never to return in such concentration ever again, fearing the wrath of the new rules and the stiffer sentences.

As I have said, no one will ever stamp the game out, and later, some of the girls drifted back, but the sights to be seen prior to 1959 have never been repeated.

Clandestine affairs of the heart, in themselves, are not unlawful, nor indeed are they any concern of the police, though they often do, come to the notice, due to the very nature of their secrecy and attempts at concealment. Sometimes, on my day off, I would leave my own police area and visit a delightful country pub, 'The Three Arrows' which stood on its own in the centre of a stretch of countryside between Bury and Heywood within the jurisdiction of the Lancashire Constabulary.

At night the area was in total darkness and the many side lanes were the resort of couples, in cars who sought to be away from public gaze. I had propped up the bar with my first pint of the evening when Tommy, mine host, joined me.

"Had a bit of disturbance Saturday night," he whispered. I told him that I was surprised as I had never heard of any trouble at the Arrows.

"No, nothing like that," he hastened to inform me. "What happened was that me and the wife were asleep and about two in the morning we woke to hear banging on the front door. Now, as you know, we're miles from civilisation and it put the wind up me. I opened the bedroom window and saw a young woman on the step, it was raining heavy and she was wet through. Well we went down and after making sure there was no one else lurking around, I let her in. Her crying, and shivering in her wet clothes, upset the wife and she took her off into the kitchen to dry out. I made some tea and about half an hour later I got the story from her, in fits and starts that is."

Tommy, after refilling my pot, went on to relate the rest of the circumstances to me. He said that he telephoned the girl's parents, who lived at Rochdale, and the police at Bury.

"But what did this girl say?" I asked. The girl, it transpired, had been to a well known dance hall in Manchester, where she had met a good looking chap in his late twenties, and at the end of the evening, having found the lad charming and attentive, had accepted his offer of a lift home. She had, apparently been a little apprehensive, but on leaving the dance hall and finding torrential rain, welcomed his polite offer.

He had told her of a short cut to her home location and she had not been too unhappy when he was driving through dark country lanes. However, when the vehicle came to a halt she became alarmed. The nice charming escort demanded that she move into the rear seat of the car and prepare for some serious lovemaking. She of course refused, and the man demanded that she leave the car immediately. She did so and when the vehicle was driven away, she was obliged to wander around in the dark and wet night, until stumbling upon 'The Three Arrows.

"And what did the cops say?" I asked, already knowing what the answer would be.

"They told her she had been a lucky girl, but as the man had not broken the law, there wasn't anything more they could do."

The unfortunate girl was collected by her parents an hour or so later and Tom went back to bed.

On the next occasion I called to see Tommy he had an almost identical story to tell. A different girl of course, but no doubt the same lover boy. I had not been to the 'Three Arrows' for a couple of months and when I popped in one Sunday lunchtime, I enquired from Tommy as to whether he was still having to take in distressed women in the middle of the night.

"Definitely not," he said. "There were two more we let in with the same tale and I think a few more knocked, but we never took any notice. Course there were weeks when no one at all disturbed us, and I think he must have been accommodated on those Saturday nights."

Unfortunately, no matter how much publicity is given, to warn girls about the schemes of evil men, they still allow themselves to be taken in by a few pretended complements and disguised interest. In most cases, a great deal of subterfuge is employed in affairs which must be kept secret, usually in an effort to conceal what is taking place from a partner or friend. About four o'clock one morning, I was informed by one of the beat men that a dead man had been found lying on a bench at a bus stop. I attended the scene and found the deceased to be around fifty years old, with no marks of violence. He had a substantial amount of cash about him, ruling out foul play and a post mortem revealed a massive heart attack had killed him. It seemed, therefore, to be a case of the poor man sitting down on the bench and passing away quite naturally. Until the night watchman from a nearby railway yard came to the station.

He had seen a black cab draw up at the stop and the driver take an apparently drunken man from the vehicle and dump him on the bench. The witness had written down the badge number of the taxi which I gratefully took into my possession. Within an hour I was interviewing the cab driver concerned.

"All I did sergeant was to help out a regular customer, a big tipper she is," he explained. The licensee of an ancient pub in the city centre, a lady, long divorced, had been entertaining one of her regulars to an after hours drink. The couple had become good friends, though the man was married and after the staff had gone home, she invited him upstairs to her bedroom, a practice which had been repeated on several occasions over the course of the past few months.

No sooner had her friend caressed her than he fell back with a groan and she realised that he had died.

"I didn't know what to do and I didn't want what had happened to get out, so I telephoned the cab rank and asked for Tony to come. Tony has been my regular cab driver for years and is very reliable. When he got here I took him straight upstairs and explained what had happened. He wasn't sure what to do, so I asked him to dress the body and take him up near where he lives." she told me.

Tony did as she requested. "I dropped him off on a seat at his local bus stop and the rest you know," said the hapless Tony.

The Coroner was made aware of all the circumstances, and no inquest was held, thereby protecting all concerned from embarrassment.

Subterfuge and cunning play a major role in secret trysts,

though caution is often cast onto the winds. I was investigating a day time burglary which had taken place in a cul-de-sac of good class detached houses and followed the usual pattern, in those days, of enquiring at every other house in the hope that someone may have witnessed something of significance. More often than not, there will be a neighbour whom the rest of the road refer unkindly to, as a nosey-parker. And that person, when identified, can be very useful to an investigation. I had visited almost all the houses in the cul-de sac before I found a lady of that awful description. She had in fact, seen nothing to help me, but did inform me of a matter of life and death, as she put it.

"That woman over the road needs a good talking to officer," she announced, pointing to the house in question. "Her husband is out at work all day and she has another man round at her house on Wednesday afternoons."

I explained that the matter was not one that the police were concerned with, but she went on.

"She meets him somewhere in her car and he climbs into the boot, then she drives straight into her garage and after she has closed the garage door, she lets him out of the boot. Afterwards, the garage doors open and she drives off to where she picks him up and lets him out of the boot. Later you see her come back to get on with her husband's tea."

As she had no information regarding the burglary I left her to continue with my house to house enquiry. When I eventually knocked at the door of the alleged adulteress I had made up my mind to broach the subject of her liaison.

"You know, if someone is locked in the boot of a car they could suffocate," I began.

The young woman sat down quickly onto an armchair with a gasp.

"What do you mean? What do you know? What's happened to Gordon?" she cried.

"Nothing has happened to Gordon, yet," I said in an attempt to set her at ease. "I am merely pointing out that should a person carrying another person in the boot of their vehicle have an accident and find themselves in hospital in an unconscious state, nobody would know about Gordon and he may be in there for days, or if your husband were to collect the car and find him in there ..."

"I understand," said the young woman as I bade her good day.

Chapter Thirteen

As I pointed out earlier, not everything that the plain-clothes department dealt with was sexually orientated. I was given the job of investigating a couple of serious woundings which had occurred on my section. Two men had entered the Ducie Arms, near to the prison and had attacked the licensee. The victim had remonstrated with the men after they had thrown the contents of their pint pots over him, and in answer to his comments, one of the men punched the landlord and broke his nose.

After the assault, the assailant and his friend visited several other public houses in the vicinity, eventually arriving at the Hightown Hotel. Here, our two friends argued with the licensee and his staff after being refused drink. One of the pair struck the licensee over the head with a soda syphon from the bar counter, causing a deep laceration to his scalp and rendering him unconscious, whilst his partner held back a couple of waiters who attempted to go to the aid of their employer.

Both complainants identified their assailants from a set of photographs I displayed to them and I consequently circulated their pictures. I was soon supplied with their addresses and having by now been informed of their extremely violent nature, made sure that my colleagues on the department accompanied me on the visit to both addresses. The man who had actually dealt the blows had, it transpired, fled to Ireland, though we were successful in detaining his accomplice.

The offence with which I charged the accomplice, was, in those days, a felony, and though the evidence was that he had not in fact actually assaulted either of the victims, he was nevertheless guilty of the wounding with which I charged him.

If, for example, a man burgled a house by breaking a window and climbing through, and his friend stood at the end of the street in order to warn him should the police be nearby, then the friend would be equally guilty of the burglary, though he was a mile away. It was described in the law, as being a principal in the felony.

The accomplice appeared at court and was remanded to prison until such time as I produced his friend. As it seemed we were never going to trace him, it was decided to go on with the trial of the 'bird in hand'.

I stepped into the witness box, and a particularly obnoxious lawyer stood up to announce that he was appearing for the defence. In those early days of my police service, my Achilles heel was that I was very young in appearance, and though I was in fact some twenty nine years of age, I looked about eighteen. The sneering barrister immediately got on to the point that his client was, on neither of the occasions, any where near the injured men. In answer, I agreed that was the case. He adjusted his gown across his shoulders and grasping his lapels, turned to the jury.

"Then will you tell the court, how it is that my client appears today, charged with wounding, when you say he was yards away when the alleged offence was committed by some other person who is not here today?"

I faced the judge and gave a full explanation, quoting the law of principals and accessories in felonies, giving the example of the burglary pair. I spoke for some twenty minutes and caught the approving gaze of the his lordship when the jury, having listened intently to my explanation, given in laymen terms, retired for a few minutes and returned with a finding of guilt. The abettor was given three years imprisonment, and some six months later, when his friend turned up, he received a seven year sentence.

The villainous barrister was a regular at the Manchester Courts and in later years, he told me that he had believed me to be a probationer constable, in civvies, probably because it was my day off, and that I would not be able to answer his question.

"I took a gamble and it didn't come off," he said.

Some years later the force adopted a scheme whereby solicitors were employed on a regular basis to represent the prosecution and the general public began to enjoy the facilities of free legal aid. This new system did away with the requirement of the officer in the case to attend the court where there was an anticipated plea of guilty. Of course those arrangements suited the police officers concerned, especially those on nights.

The detectives, however, came up against a devious practice, which created a lot of unnecessary paper work and hindered their getting out to investigate a heavy load of crime. Often, when an individual had been charged with a crime, he would accept that the evidence weighed so heavily against him, that there was no point in attempting to deny it to the court. He would inform the detective in the case that it would be his intention to plead guilty at his first appearance, and convey the same decision to the charge office sergeant, who would endorse the charge sheet accordingly.

Many miscreants would further, volunteer a written statement to that effect and sign it.

On their appearance at court, they would be offered the free representation of their case by a lawyer who had been retained under the legal aid scheme. Of course the officer in the case was not there to point out that the man had indicated his wish to be thrown to the mercy of the bench with his honest confession. At that stage, the solicitor designated to prosecute the case, would have not yet seen the accused, so the way was clear. The fee collected by the legal aid counsellor for a single appearance, something around eighty pounds in those days, could be doubled by the simple advice to the client, to plead not guilty, ask for an adjournment, and on the second appearance, advise the bewildered crook to then change his plea to one of guilty, thereby picking up a hundred and sixty pounds.

Of course not every legal aid defence lawyer was unscrupulous by any means, but when they were, the hapless detective, having been given notice of the surprise 'not guilty' plea, was obliged to stop whatever he was doing and prepare a file for the court and the prosecuting solicitor. That duty involved tracing any witnesses, obtaining lengthy statements from them and having the whole thing typed up, a task which could take a week or more to complete, during which time, all the other crimes taking place on his patch went undetected, all that in the knowledge that it was unnecessary.

Sometimes I have attended the Crown Court, where a genuine 'not guilty' was to be heard, only to discover that the prosecuting barrister has not even looked at the brief, it only having been passed to him immediately preceding the trial by his firm. On those occasions I have had to go through the whole of the evidence with them, having only minutes to do so before the accused is called and then to hurry out of the courtroom to await my summons to the witness box.

Then there were those annoying deals that defence and prosecution lawyers regularly hatched. The police officer who had worked very hard, in difficult and often dangerous circumstances, to gather sufficient evidence, often over a long period of time, would attend the hearing, only to discover that the lawyers had agreed together to strike one of those bargains.

My first experience of that sort of skullduggery was an occasion where I had charged a particularly vicious individual with an assault occasioning actual bodily harm, an offence for which the perpetrator may be punished with five years imprisonment. His victim had been receiving the appropriate treatment in hospital for three weeks and was now ready to appear before the Magistrates Court, hopefully to see his assailant sent on to a higher court for trial. Other prosecution witnesses arrived, as arranged, and we were all assembled outside, waiting to be called to give evidence.

The prosecuting solicitor approached me and informed me that he and the villain's counsel had agreed that the accused could plead guilty to common assault. That the case was over and the man had been bound over for twelve months, meaning that if he avoided prosecution for assaulting people over the ensuing year, that would have been an end to it. I told him what I thought of him, as did several of the witnesses, not least the chap who still bore the marks of the attack.

The agreement had been quite legally affected and it meant less fuss for both lawyers, probably to accommodate some private arrangement between them. The freed thug carried on beating people with impunity and not having been charged over that year, went on doing so for a long time after.

Sometimes it was suggested to me that it would be much more effective to make one's own arrangements in order to ensure that criminals were punished sufficiently in order to persuade them, and others, that you would prefer them to leave you out of their nefarious activities once and for all. I saw the value of that suggestion when the proprietor of a night club, come music hall, having been plagued with persons breaking into his premises and they, being frustrated in their search for cash, resorting to causing the utmost damage to furniture in the club, that he sought a solution other than a recourse to the law.

"You buggers," he said to me one evening when I called to see him at the nationally acclaimed club, "can't seem to catch the bastards that are breaking in here and it's beyond a joke now."

I took a swig from the glass of ale passed to me from the bar and offered a little unofficial advice.

"You know that woman that's always ringing us about the noise outside this place." I ventured.

"The old bag over the road?"

"Yes," I said. I was aware that the dear lady in question made a habit of watching the side door of the club and the street outside it at all hours. "Why don't you go over and ask her to write down anything she sees that would indicate who it is that keeps breaking in?" I went on, advising him to take her a case of stout so that she might refresh herself during her vigil. I advised him that should she come up with anything tangible, he would do well to contact a certain firm in the Liverpool area, who would help him out.

I saw him some months later and asked him whether the nosey parker had come up with anything.

"She sure did. I had yet another break-in and all the one-arm bandits were smashed. I went over and asked if she had written anything down. She said there was no need because it was two men who were well known in the district." he said.

I asked him what happened then. "I rang that scouse firm and heard that the bastards what was doing all the break-ins had gone to hospital with broken limbs and all that," he beamed.

"Cost me a few quid, but it was well worth it. The word goes round you know."

I did know. The club is still there to this day and still in the family, and has never had a burglary in the last forty odd years.

Chapter Fourteen

Those fashionable methods employed by outlaws in the nineteen fifties and sixties, which enabled them to withdraw cash from banks, without the inconvenience of opening an account, has, in these latter years, declined in popularity. The days when these halls of finance were vulnerable in the extreme are over, and like places of worship, sophisticated devices have had to be installed, in the recognition that nothing is any longer sacred.

In those years long ago, when the occasional bank employee gave way to temptation and somehow managed to get their own money mixed up with that of the bank, their employers would deal with the matter, without recourse to the police or the courts. That was done so as not to frighten customers into believing that their money wasn't so safe as they had been led to believe. Some crimes however, were so serious as to force those institutions to bring in the police.

One humid night in the late fifties, I came on duty at the Cheetham Hill Police Station and was ordered to go at once to bank premises in the main shopping street where I was to relieve the afternoon officer who had been there since the early evening.

On my arrival, the other constable mumbled something about not having had any supper and brushed past me towards the direction of the station, no explanation was offered as to why I was there. I closed the door and found that I was in the living quarters of the establishment and alone.

All the lights were on and I set off along a corridor to what I could see was the kitchen. I called out, just to verify that there were no other persons around. There was no reply and I began to experience a strange eerie feeling.

I looked around and on the wall behind the door of the kitchen were several bloodstains. Near to those were marks in the door jamb, obviously made by someone hitting the area with an axe. A look around in the bedrooms on the upper floor, revealed more extensive bloodstains, some being those of an adult whilst others were of a child.

A double bed was soaked in congealed blood and there were many more axe marks on the walls and doors. A telephone lay smashed in the lounge area, where there were more signs of blood and damaged furniture. I returned to the kitchen and made myself comfortable in a chair. The eerie silence of the place was suddenly dispelled by the refrigerator motor starting up and causing me to jump out of my skin.

Relieved by a colleague at two in the morning, I learnt that the manager of the bank had murdered his mother-in-law and his baby daughter and had seriously wounded his wife.

"He tried to finish himself off after by ramming a carving knife into his chest and falling on it. Didn't succeed though, he's in Crumpsall Hospital under guard. Have you brewed up?"

I told him that I hadn't, then left him to do that very thing at the station. Later it was alleged that the manager had been systematically embezzling the bank and knowing of an imminent audit, he followed what he saw as his only course of action. A few months after the affair, the bank was again the scene of skullduggery, when two men kept watch on three consecutive Fridays, when a local businessman made a habit of parking outside the premises, leaving his vehicle and entering the bank carrying a large brief case.

On the fourth Friday they watched him go into the building, and when he came out, they pounced on him, grabbed the bag and made off. They had patiently observed their quarry for four weeks as he carried substantial amounts of cash into the bank, and in the belief that the opposite was the case, they succeeded in stealing an old and battered brief case.

Another bank in the district, offered the facility of after hours depositing. On the wall of the building there was a sliding door to which the customer had a key and it was common to see a queue of shopkeepers along the front of the premises in the late evening, as they pushed their day's takings through the wall safe. The idea was, that the various deposits would be credited to the client's account on the following morning, or in the case of Saturday's takings, on Monday.

One dark evening at the height of Christmas trading, the depositors arrived at the hole in the wall, to discover a notice which informed them that the deposit safe was out of order and drawing attention to a formidable temporary box adjacent to the faulty one. The notice was to the effect that whilst their keys were of no use, the temporary box was backed by a chute which was designed to carry their cash along to the vault where it would be secure until the next day of business.

Most of those making use of the facility, were junior members of staff, who were anxious to catch their buses and complied with the notice, shoving their precious loads into the box and scampering away. The large and impressive receptacle and its overflowing load was gone within the hour and was never traced, nor was the perpetrator ever detected.

The idea, unfortunately, caught on, and was practised all over the city on a number of occasions going undetected. King Street in the city centre, lined on both sides with the main banks, came under criminal activity also, though nothing of a violent nature, such as armed hold-ups.

So important was the security of these businesses that the police provided street patrols all day. The dedicated officers who carried out these patrols were in fact members of the police band and as such, could not be employed on anything other than regular day duties. The normal beats operated on a shift system and in consequence, bandsmen never appeared on the rota. It was, between band performances and interminable practise sessions that those officers guarded the city banks. During the latter part of the nineteen sixties, King Street became the hunting place of a particularly cool thief.

This enterprising villain, described as middle aged, smart appearance, in a dark business suit and horn rimmed spectacles, had noticed that it was the practice for many of the city firms to send the office junior, very often a boy or girl of only fourteen years of age, along to one or other of the banks to collect, often, large sums of cash.

The *modus operandi* of the well-dressed confidence trickster, was to stop these youngsters as they left a bank and introduce himself as the bank manager. He would tell the boy, or girl, that his staff had inadvertently handed them the wrong package of money, take it from them asking that they wait whilst he brought the correct package out to them.

The hapless juvenile would hang around until it became obvious that he wasn't appearing and subsequently return to their employee empty handed.

The con-man made a habit of perpetrating his crimes in other cities, appearing on crime bulletins from time to time. He successfully visited Manchester on numerous occasions over some five or six years and despite the dedicated efforts of the bandsmen to detect him, he was never caught and he probably retired to the countryside.

Maybe, when relaxing in the evening, he listens to his collection of records, made by the Band Of The Manchester City Police.

Despite all these trials and tribulations, there were periods when one could get away from it all albeit it was difficult to completely relax. Later on in my service, when it became possible to obtain a mortgage, most of us moved out into the suburbs and beyond. Those moves brought the luxury of having spent eight hours or more in some crap district, driving home and seeing the quality of the areas through which you travelled, gradually improving, and arriving at the lovely decent area you had chosen to hang a millstone around your neck for.

A fellow sergeant and his wife invited my wife and I to accompany them on a weekend visit to the home of their friends in Cheshire.

"He's that doctor I told you about," said my colleague.

"The one who's in practice with the doctor from Ireland?" I enquired. Tony, my friend, affirmed that it was, and on the following Friday we drove over to a lovely village in the south of Cheshire, arriving at the large ivy covered house which combined the surgery with our host's living quarters.

Following introductions, the doctor told us that his colleague had been called to Ireland as a relative had become seriously ill.

"Means we can't go for a meal in Chester I'm afraid," he announced.

His wife explained that her husband now having to see his partner's patients at the evening surgery, as well as his own, would make it somewhere around eight-thirty before he could be finished.

"I booked a table at the golf club for eight and now I'll have to cancel it," said our hostess. My pal, Tony, was one of those naturally distinguished looking men, always, as on this occasion, immaculately turned out and having a front which was bigger than the one at Blackpool.

"Why don't you see some of the patients, then we could be in time for the reserved table?" I asked, jokingly.

The doctor's wife said it could be done, and I contributed that it was a well known fact that a lot of people went through life enjoying bad health and attending surgeries when there was nothing wrong with them.

"You're right about that," said the doctor.

"Well, Tony could see the hypochondriacs in your colleagues office, whilst you saw the genuine bunch," I suggested.

Everyone looked at everyone else, then we all looked at the physician, whose wife said it could be done and the die was cast. The doctor made a list of those who could safely be seen by Tony, who sat behind the desk in preparation to offering advice to the waiting crowd outside.

There was a button on the desk, which he pressed to announce that the first patient was to enter the office. It was a woman who told him of sleepless nights, constant headaches and a loss of appetite, all since her husband had left her for a young girl he had met at work.

He listened patiently for some fifteen minutes, then told her to drink six pints of water every day. He told each of the people to drink that amount of water every day, until at long last, he had seen all the people allocated to his surgery.

The real doctor, having cleared his patients at around the same time, joined him in the house, and we left in plenty of time to claim the reservation at the golf club. It was altogether a great weekend which sealed a friendship destined to last for many years.

Some time after doctor Tony's administrations, he was informed that many of the people seen by him on that Friday, had asked when that tall good looking doctor would be there again, as they had felt so well after seeing him.

"Whitehall," said one of my favourite inspectors, "is where the civil servants produce all this bloody legislation that we have to keep abreast of." I was deep into twelve months of study in an effort to gain success in the forthcoming promotion examinations, and found that almost as quickly as I had absorbed an Act of Parliament, an amendment to several of its sections would appear. These amendments appeared to me to be unnecessary, changing a phrase or a word here and there as though it had been an afterthought.

"Well that's because of the public school system," sighed the inspector. "See, when the people who are out of the top drawer have a son born, they enrol the kid into Eton or Harrow immediately. When they do that the headmaster asks them what they want the lad to be, and if they choose the civil service, that's what he would be trained for from day one." I asked what happened if the child didn't want to be what his parents required, or if he wasn't up to all the academic work.

"Got to do as he is told. Of course if he is not up to it with regard to the lessons, or a card short in the pack, they put him in the army or the church."

"So all the blokes in Westminster, apart from elected MPs are there permanently?" I said.

"That's it, they sit around in posh offices all day with a pencil and paper, and they can either play at noughts and crosses or alter any recently produced acts of parliament," said the inspector.

It certainly appeared to me that many of the amendments were entirely the work of someone employed as the inspector was suggesting, though other pieces of the statutes carried no clues as to the soundness of mind of their author .

In 1780 the Sunday Observance Act became law. A place used for public entertainment on a Sunday and persons were admitted on payment, became a disorderly house, and the keeper of such a place faced punishment of a fine of two hundred pounds, an astronomical sum in those days. Nonpayment of the fine within fourteen days resulted in a prison sentence and a closing down of the premises. You might think that by the nineteen seventies, an old law like that would have long since passed into oblivion, but I was to discover that, due to the influence of a group of dedicated people, called the Lord's Day Observance Society, it was very much alive and kicking. I have never been able to discover why minority groups hold such sway, whilst the views of the majority are ignored.

The superintendent sent for me on a Saturday morning, saying he had a job for me the next day. He showed me a letter under the heading of the Lord's Day Observance Society, the contents of which described a set of observations taken by their members on four consecutive Sundays prior to the date of the letter. There was the revelation that at one of the pubs in Longsight, a pianist was engaged on Sunday evenings to lead community singing by customers who packed the place from seven to ten.

One of the observers had gleaned from the pianist, and a singer, that they had been engaged on a professional basis, for a small fee. I was instructed to go along with a couple of constables, and if the allegations were true, to report the licensee for any offences revealed.

The next evening we turned up at the pub, in plain-clothes, and sure enough the complainants were correct in their painstaking evidence. The singer was belting out an old favourite of mine, 'There's an old mill by the stream Nellie Dean,' whilst most of the happy audience joined in, and there were some signs of disagreement when I took the microphone to announce that they were breaking the law.

"We've paid fifty pence to come in," was a popular cry as I closed the lid of the piano. I informed the landlord that I was reporting him for summons and with a heavy heart, I left the scene.

Like most coppers, I had sympathy for many of the people I had to deal with, certainly towards the crowd in that pub who were merely enjoying a well earned relaxation before returning to another week of hard work, probably of a boring nature. But the law is the law, and when anyone brings a violation of that law to the attention of the police authority, then it must be investigated, or at least that was the case those many years ago.

1974 found me turned out to grass as the divisional Crime Prevention Officer. That job, one of the best duties in the bobbies, was a very good way of winding down. Nine to five and weekends off for the last year of my service, it was an insight to better things. The lads gave me a terrific send off at a local C.I.D. pub, and presented me with an impressive set of glass table wear, which, being under the influence of a large amount of alcohol, I dropped whilst attempting to get out of a taxi outside my home.

A few days after my retirement, I met an old customer of mine, whom I had sent to prison some years previously. I bought him a pint and we shook hands as he wished me a happy retirement.

"I keep out of trouble these days Dennis," he said. "Any way it was all just a simple game we were playing."

He was right, it was just a game.

" After all," I told him, "If it wasn't for the likes of you my friend, I'd have been out of work!"